Praise for Asha
You Are the Medicine

"*You Are the Medicine* is a profound and beautifully written book offered by Indigenous Medicine Woman Asha Frost. With a sensitive lyricism and nuance in her writing she shares stories inspired by her Ojibway ancestry following the lunar calendar of 13 moons. This book reveals how to claim our inherent capacity for healing in all ways. Inviting us to connect to our own ancestral wisdom by sharing hers, she generously and lovingly shows us the way home. A must read for our times."

—Colette Baron-Reid, Author and Oracle Creator

"I have deep respect for Asha Frost and the sacred work she does. In *You Are the Medicine*, Asha takes us on a journey sharing deep wisdom through mesmerising storytelling and embodied wisdom. Through rituals and sacred journeys she then lovingly guides us to recover the power and beauty of our own ancestral lineages. This beautiful book will breathe life into your soul and reconnect you to the medicine that has always been whispering within."

— Rebecca Campbell, Best-selling Author, Mystic, and Mother

"There is an unmistakable magic about Asha Frost—she is soft yet strong, fierce yet loving. This book is not only an honouring of sacred ancestry it also shares a tender yet deep respect for the Earth and her medicine while guiding us to authentically own who we are in a way that is in alignment with our roots. This work will initiate great healing and inspire essential change in your life."

—Kyle Gray, Best-selling Author of *Raise Your Vibration* and *Angel Prayers*

"Asha is a brilliant force of love and healing, and her ability to help others connect to their own innate medicine feels like a gift from Spirit."

— Chris-Anne Donnelly, Creator of *The Sacred Creator's Oracle* and *The Light Seer's Tarot*

"This book contains the cure to what ails us in these times: disconnection and having forgotten who we are. Allow yourself to be taken on this transformative journey to remembering who you are, what you came here for, and how to access your power anytime, anywhere, anyplace."

—Kate Northrup, Best-selling Author of *Do Less*

"*You Are the Medicine* is an act of great, and maybe undeserved, generosity. If you are interested in including activism and decolonization work as a part of your spiritual practice, Asha Frost leads you into the potency of her Indigenous culture while also guiding and imploring you to reckon with the implications of the borrowing."

— Kimberly Ann Johnson, Somatic Experiencing Practitioner, Sexological Bodyworker, Birth Doula, and Author of *Call of The Wild*

"No matter who you are, you need this book. We are all searching for healing, to remember that we are indeed our own best medicine. Asha is the perfect guide to take our hand and lead us back home to ourselves, to help us ask brave questions and step forward with courage. I hope you'll buy this book and begin the journey of becoming who you were sacredly created to be. I'll be returning to Asha's teaching again and again."

—Kaitlin Curtice, Author of *Native*

"This book is a gift to the world. It carries the voice and vision of the Ancestors. It is a portal that offers an invitation for each reader to reclaim the Medicine within. Do yourself a favor and pick up this treasure today! So grateful *You Are the Medicine* exists!"

— Christine Gutierrez, Licensed Psychotherapist, Speaker, Author of *I am Diosa*

"Asha Frost is a thought-leader anchored in her Indigenous spiritual tradition for our times. Her book and her work is a shining light for us to follow as we navigate a loss of meaning and a heartbreaking, confusing world. She guides us back to purpose with so much clarity as she invites us into reflection, ritual, story and journeying. Thank you Asha for this gift. We listen and receive."

— Susanna Barkataki, Speaker, Yoga Culture Advocate, Author of *Embrace Yoga's Roots*

"*You Are the Medicine* contains a special kind of magic comprised of honesty, generosity, and brilliant light. It is both a first step toward reconciliation and a gift to those of us who want to heal our broken places and find a more authentic way to live. With wisdom, bravery and profound kindness, Asha Frost steps into the role of Medicine Woman for us all— right when we need her most. This book provided me with an essential education not just on the soul-restoring ways of Indigenous people, but also on truths long-buried that must be brought to light. I'm grateful it was written, and know it is a book I will return to again and again."

—Marissa Stapley, Internationally Best-selling Author of *Lucky*

"An instant classic. Wise woman, Asha Frost, poetically weaves soul medicine, personal story, and sacred practice into an offering you'll turn to again and again. Asha is more than a gifted healer who has spent years cultivating her wisdom and magic; she is a bridge. She generously shares potent wisdom from her lineage guiding us to the place we all long to go: that powerful and unbroken place within ourselves. Vibrating with ancestral power and love, *You Are the Medicine* invites us to activate the self-knowing and potential for healing we already possess. Be prepared, this book will change you in all the right ways. Asha is a wonder, this book is a wonder, and we are blessed to have them both."

—Robyn Moreno, Curandera and Storyteller

"*You Are the Medicine* gently and oh-so-powerfully will awaken you to the truth of Who You Are. The reckless exploitation and destruction of the precious living resources of the Earth; colonization and oppression that left many a generation carrying deep wounds and passing them along to their children; the experience of disconnection feeding a deep mental health crisis and its tragic consequences. Waking up to the Truth of Who You Are is the medicine the world needs. It's the medicine you need. All of us do. Asha Frost walks with us on this journey as a friend and a wise guide. With each page, taking us deeper to our own Truth."

—Valerie Rein, Ph.D., Author of *Patriarchy Stress Disorder*

"Asha's words in *You Are the Medicine* touched my heart. Her own vulnerability invited me to acknowledge and embrace my own. When she shared her medicine as taught to her by her elders, she made me remember the medicine I learned from mine and called me to explore my history even deeper. Her pride in her culture made me reconnect with the pride I have in my own. By sharing the heartbreaking history of her people, I was invited to confront my own biases and commit to help build the systems where everyone can feel safe and at peace being who they are. I recommend this reading for anyone looking to reconnect deeper with themselves and their medicine. I am so grateful for Asha's light."

— Sandra Hinojosa Ludwig, Coach and Author of *Chica, Why Not?*

"When you first meet Asha Frost, you feel her vast, wise, kindness. This is the energy she brings into *You Are the Medicine* where she shares her ancestral Medicine of the Star Nations, Animal Spirits, and plant/ elementals of the Anishinaabe Ojibwe, Star People. Asha asks you to be an ally, to not only take in the beauty of these Medicines, but to also hold space for the pain. *You Are the Medicine* is a must-read for folx who find themselves on a healing, starseed path desiring to reroot into the ancestral Medicine already residing in your bones."

— Leslie Tagorda, Brand Astrologer and Author of *Star Powered Brand*

"The book you hold in your hands is more than a collection of words and chapters. It is also not a self-help book. Asha weaved together her deep knowledge, lived experience, and ancestral guidance to provide the medicine you need so you reconnect with the version of you that's beyond labels and roles. Each word written is like an invitation into becoming a better ancestor."

—Leesa Renée Hall, Mental Wellness Advocate and Anti-Bias Facilitator

YOU ARE THE
MEDICINE

YOU ARE THE
MEDICINE

13 Moons of Indigenous
Wisdom, Ancestral Connection,
and Animal Spirit Guidance

ASHA FROST

HAY HOUSE, INC.
Carlsbad, California • New York City
London • Sydney • New Delhi

Published in the United States by: Hay House, Inc.: www.hayhouse
.com® • **Published in Australia by:** Hay House Australia Pty. Ltd.: www
.hayhouse.com.au • **Published in the United Kingdom by:** Hay House UK,
Ltd.: www.hayhouse.co.uk • **Published in India by:** Hay House Publishers
India: www.hayhouse.co.in

Cover illustration: Steph Littlebird
Interior design: Julie Davison
Turtle illustration: Kai Söderström

Cataloging-in-Publication Data is on file at the Library of Congress

Tradepaper ISBN: 978-1-4019-6350-7
E-book ISBN: 978-1-4019-6351-4
Audiobook ISBN: 978-1-4019-6358-3
14 13 12 11 10 9 8 7 6 5
1st edition, March 2022

Printed in the United States of America

To Kai and Elias

May my words remind you to claim your
Indigenous presence as you continue to make
our Ancestors proud. You will always
and forever be the ones who remind
me that I'm made of Stardust.

CONTENTS

INTRODUCTION

Aaniin, Boozhoo, Hello. I believe that we dreamed of each other here.

I have a recurring vision in which I'm standing on the shores of *Gitche Namay Weeqadoong*, the Georgian Bay, on *Neyaashiinigmiing*, my home territory, and I'm watching, listening. I am wearing buckskin, and my hair is braided. This vision transcends time, though it somehow lives in my bone memory.

I see you in a boat coming to the shore and looking to settle here. I welcome you with an open heart and arms, for you are my Kin, and I want to develop a relationship with you. I stand here with a generous and humble Spirit. I am not sure of your intentions, but I know that we are here to build something together. I see myself inviting you onto the Land, and as I do, I shift into my Medicine Woman self, offering you my hand, for I know that we are here for healing, reconciliation, and repair. You are my *Niiji*: my friend.

This book is part of this dream for I am a Rainbow Bridge. My Spirit name is Healing Rainbow Woman, my lineage is Anishinaabe, and I hold space for a healed vision. Walking in both worlds, Spirit and Earth, modern and traditional, one foot in each world, I'm here to trailblaze and activate, remembering for all who come into my sacred space.

The Anishinaabe people refer to three tribes: Ojibwe, Potawatomi, and Odawa. I am a member of the Ojibwe people, currently living on the Lands of the Anishinaabe, Huron-Wendat, and Haudenosaunee. My Ancestors come from Anishinaabe territories across what is now known as Ontario, Canada.

As you begin this book, take a moment to acknowledge the traditional Lands you are on. If you don't know whose lands you occupy, this is a perfect time to find out. You can look it up at native-land.ca—this incredible resource covers all of Turtle Island. As you acknowledge the Earth beneath your feet, feel the Spirit of the Land and all it carries, for it has witnessed lifetimes of both beauty and pain. Land acknowledgments remind everyone of the truth that we, Indigenous people, are still here. When spoken with intention, the words remind all who listen that no one can erase our colonial and oppressive history. As Indigenous people, we place ourselves in relationship to the Land; we don't own it—we have a kinship with it. When we speak these words, we acknowledge the broken treaties and the repair that is needed. Land acknowledgments are so much more than words spoken; they create ripples of healing past, present, and future.

As you acknowledge the Land on which you stand, feel into your own lineage. Envision your roots reaching into the spaces and places your Ancestors lived, the spaces where your Medicines originate. Bring them forward today, dear *Niiji*, for I value your power and presence here.

For lifetimes, Indigenous people have known the power of Earth and Spirit Medicine. Everything in our natural world is interconnected and viewed as sacred. Since time immemorial, we have developed a reciprocal relationship with the Earth, our Ancestors, and the Spirit World. The Plants, Animals, Rocks, Waters, Stars, and Moon are our Relations, our

Kin. We love them as our relatives, deserving of deep respect and honor. Every aspect of Creation has a Spirit. This Spirit lives in all things and informs us how to walk in a good way— *Mino-bimaadiziwin*. Spirit-to-Spirit connection brings us back to the knowledge that we are all divine beings walking in a balanced relationship with one another.

As an Indigenous Medicine Woman working with folks for almost two decades, I have encountered many people searching for a deeper connection to Earth Medicine ways and Indigenous teachings. Our practices, beliefs, and ways of living have deep roots, and it is my experience that those searching for healing find solace and transformation in our ancient wisdom. Those who come to me for healing have felt disconnected from their purpose, ancestry, and power. I have found that Indigenous teachings act as a catalyst to awaken their remembering of who they are and why they are here.

You Are the Medicine is a prayer to your inner wisdom. The words you will read through this book are intended to activate your knowing. I believe that you have lifetimes of experience, soul essence, and Medicine power vibrating within your cells. Your Ancestors dreamed you here, and you are ready to remember all that you came to be. You carry the Medicines of the many who have walked before you, a divine presence that is like no other upon this great Earth.

Throughout our time together, I will share some words from my Ojibwe language, Anishiinabemowin. The impact of residential schools, oppression, and colonization runs deep. I don't know how to speak my language fluently, but the words I share here are filled with reclamation and remembering. I could never fully understand your path, but maybe you, too, have experienced the call to reclaim lost and forgotten pieces of the past.

As I write this, more than 1,300 forgotten graves from the children who died in residential schools across our country have been found, with more to come. I will be speaking about the horrors of residential schools later in this book. These children never got to be Elders, Storytellers, Medicine People, Wisdom Carriers. *You Are the Medicine* is written for these invisible voices who now live in the Spirit World. The forgotten children guide me to write these words, so that their presence can be brought into the light.

As we open this Sacred Space together, my Ancestors gather. They have been waiting, for they have been accustomed to having their voices silenced, their Indigenous existence diminished. This book is here to bring visibility to the voices in my bones and the songs in my womb. My Ancestors are ready to share their healing ways through my words, and they offer a prayer that you will use them in a good way. As Indigenous people, we see the sacredness that circles hold. It is a primary symbol in nature; the Sun, the Moon, life cycles, and so much more reflect this wholeness. Envision that we are all seated in circle, for this is the best way for Medicine to be shared. When we sit in this way, we truly see one another.

SHAKING UP THE TRUTH

Over my lifetime as an Indigenous woman, I have heard many ignorant and unconscious statements: "I wish I could have a status card like you!" "You're so smart for an Indian." "My BFF is my Spirit Animal." "Why can't I dress up like a sexy Pocahontas?" A few years ago, before the deepest dive into my personal healing work around my identity, every time someone made a statement like these examples, my body would start to shake. I was shaking from holding in years of trauma caused by stealing, oppression, and colonizing inflicted on generations upon generations. My cells, blood, and bone marrow knew. A body—your body—always knows. I started to realize that these words were activating intergenerational trauma—the inherited transmission of the pain of my Ancestors through my very own genes and cellular memory.

I saw mostly white women taking our Medicines and not honoring them properly, waving sage on Instagram ads for sales or posting naked photos of themselves wearing Headdresses. I started to see that they wanted to take everything they considered beautiful as their own and leave all the trauma and truth behind. It had taken me years to feel worthy enough to just stand in who I was, to heal through feelings of unworthiness to practice my own culture. There were so many layers of shame to move through before I could step up and out. Grief and anger began to rise in me.

Why weren't these people also sharing the truth? Why weren't they raising awareness to the generational impact of trying to "strip the Indian out of the child" by taking family and love away from the most innocent? Why weren't they sharing about the missing and murdered Indigenous Women and Two-Spirit folks? Why weren't they talking about the youth dying from suicide and the mental health crises in our community? What about the lack of clean Water on First Nation Land? It was easy for them to take and then profit off our Medicines without holding the whole story. It was easy for them to look away.

One day, the shaking became too much. I remember I was on the phone with a friend and she asked me if it was time to get this out of my body. She reflected to me how often I had called her in tears, feeling this whole-body tremor. I agreed; it was time to speak. I wrote a letter to white women that went viral. I intended to heal my Spirit and Body, but it touched the collective more deeply than I had ever imagined it would. It caused disruption, anger, and defensiveness. And it also created healing, listening, and leaning in. My inbox and DMs filled with hundreds of messages both of support and disparagement. Many people wanted to share their personal stories around trauma, past lives, and lineages. It taught me so much about both the power and challenges that come from speaking your truth. I want to share that I use the term "white woman" because this is my reality. It isn't women of color who are causing harm; it is white women. I know that this term can be triggering for folks, yet people call me "Indigenous woman" all the time. Please try to see that I am simply calling in those who were causing pain to Indigenous people by taking and benefiting from our Medicines.

In our current climate, conversations around the harm of appropriation are vital for true reconciliation, equity, and healing. I share these conversations here because if non-Indigenous folks want to learn about and use Indigenous teachings, it's essential to be equally invested in learning about how colonization, oppression, and racism have affected our people. I understand why folks want to learn about our Medicine ways. They are so beautiful and filled with so much depth and connection. Our heritage is filled with richness, tradition, and teachings that continue to connect us to Earth and Spirit. The intention of my letter was not to tell people to turn away from our Medicines and teachings; rather it was an invitation to come in closer and really see Indigenous people and the issues that we deal with in the present day. I believe we can hold both.

Working on this book two years after sharing that letter, I can reflect on how much has healed in me. It's truth that has been carried in my bones and body. For so long, it has felt heavy to carry. I have carried it as a responsibility to my Ancestors and recently during a healing session; they told me that it was time for me to walk in freedom. In order for me to do that, I need to acknowledge that I am ready for you, dear reader, to carry a piece too. Perhaps the words will help us walk in reconciliation together; perhaps they will open your heart to Indigenous lives or maybe they will plant a seed of how we can bring more love to this great Earth we call home. I share this letter as a Sacred Space opening. It is not how one would traditionally open space, but because we need truth before we can reconcile, it feels vital to do it in this way.

The Fire is lit.

The Ancestors are here.

Your Medicine is calling.

Let us open our space.

Leave safety behind. Put your body on the line.
Stand before the people you fear and
speak your mind—even if your voice shakes.

— MAGGIE KUHN

THE LETTER

Dear White Woman who wants to be like me,

I get it. You see the moccasins and the beaded earrings. The cheekbones and the drum. The smudge bowl and the feathers.

It all looks so exotic. Something that you want to be a part of. Something you want to consume.

And you think that maybe if you borrow a few of these things, you too can connect to the Earth more deeply, to the Ancestral wisdom, to the Spirit World.

I've heard it time and time again. "I wish I was you." "I would LOVE to be Native." "You are so lucky." "I was Native in a past life." "I really want a status card, and I think I have Native blood. Can you tell me how to get one?"

Again and again, I've heard these things from you. And my heart pains. And my throat closes, and my tears get swallowed.

Do you really know what you're saying? Do you really know what you're asking for?

I love my heritage. I am proud of who I am. Even when I wear my beaded earrings and people whisper behind my back, asking, "Who does she think she is?" Even when I walk in my mukluks and teenagers shout Indian calls at me. Even when I'm discriminated against when I enter the hospital.

I love who I am. I am a proud Anishinaabe, Ojibwe Woman.

And it's taken me 42 years to get here.

So, dear White Woman, I want to ask you this: I know that you would take on the Dreamcatchers and the pow wows. I know that you would take on the Headdress and the Sage. I know that you would take on the wisdom and the beauty.

But do you want the rest of it?

Truly?

Would you like to experience people asking to collaborate with you so they can receive grants intended for Indigenous creators for their work?

Would you like to be seen and treated as less than when you have pneumonia and are in desperate need of hospital care?

Asked by medical professionals how much alcohol you've had to drink when all you need is medicine?

Would you like to have big dreams and wonder every single day whether you will be able to rise in this current system?

Would you like to feel physically ill every time you read the comments section and see the horrible views society has about your people?

Would you like to shake violently afterward and wonder if you and your children are safe in this world?

Would you take on a painful chronic illness and later wonder if part of the reason you have it is due to the oppression and pain your people have experienced?

Would you take all of this on too?

I look around at a world that has reduced me to a costume. A world that has romanticized me into a character. A world that takes the teachings of my people and uses them without any acknowledgment or an invitation for us to join them on their stage.

This is the world we live in.

And so, dear White Woman who wants to be like me:

Are you willing to take on all of it?

Or just the pretty parts?

YOU ARE THE MEDICINE

Are you willing to take on the trauma?

Or just the wisdom?

Are you willing to deal with the intergenerational trauma of the residential schools and the alcohol and the suicide and the violence and the genocide?

Are you willing to carry all of that in your cells, your blood, your tissue? Ready to do the work every single day to heal this so you can make sure your children don't carry it as you have?

Dear White Woman who wants to be like me:

Do you?

Or can you be like you, and reconnect to your own sacred Medicines? Your own beautiful ancestry? Your own power, presence, and brilliance?

I see you wanting to. I see you aspiring to. I see you reconnecting.

Can you be like you?

As I reclaim and remember me.

And then, we can finally walk in right relation to each other.

Miigwetch,
Nenaandawi Nagweyaab Kwe
Healing Rainbow Woman

> **Medicine Reflection:** How does this letter touch you? What rises for you? Can you stay with it?

MEDICINE CONNECTION

Conventionally, medicine is something you take as a substance, perhaps in a pill form or cream or tincture. It's the treatment or the prevention of disease. In my ways of knowing, Medicine is the vital, healing energy that connects the Spirit, mind, and emotional bodies. It's something carried by all living things. It is our connection, our roots, and our life force. When we return to the Medicine within ourselves and all of our Relations, we come home. We find peace, acceptance, grace, and love. Medicine is something we all carry, birthed from our Ancestors and held by our Spirit.

I believe that we all come here onto this Earth with a particular presence and soul signature. It has been my experience that when people can identify their Medicine and root into it, they rise into the path they are meant to live. Your power has always been within, and sometimes, all you need is a catalyst to remind you. This incentive to heal may come through trauma or a significant life event, as these situations tend to crack us open to discover our most profound, resilient knowing. It doesn't always have to come this way, however. I intend for this book to help you come home to the remembering that lives within your blood and bones. Through the teachings, reflection questions, rituals, and journeys may you awaken to the inherent wisdom that has always flowed through you. Your Ancestors and Guides are waiting with open arms to welcome you home so you may walk with loving connection.

Traditionally, we passed teachings down to the next generation orally, through storytelling. We shared legends of how things came to be in the natural world; our tales are woven with the Spirits of the Animal People, Plant People, Tree People, and Stone People. All aspects of Creation are alive in these legends. Teaching through stories lives deep within my lineage, and I have seen how stories can be a powerful way to inform, reveal, and stimulate inner wisdom. You will find such stories in this book, and I have intentionally infused them with activation energy. May they help you remember you carry deep Medicine, you are here for a purpose, and you have so much more within you than you ever imagined.

You may have experienced this way of learning before. When someone shares a story and it warms your heart or it feels synchronistic or like memory revisited—that is the power of storytelling. Perhaps it awakens and activates a part of your own lived experience, or maybe it's a feeling, much like déjà vu. It is a practice to notice when this happens in your life. For the folks I work with, they often get clear visions of understanding, intense sensations in their physical bodies, tears running down their face, or an expansion of joy or peace.

Our conditioning teaches us that learning must come from specific sources only. While there is certainly nothing wrong with higher education and academia, this is not the only way to learn. Indigenous people have other traditional forms of knowledge as well as a deep and profound connection to many aspects of the natural world. We use our dreams, stories, visions, senses, and connection to the Land and the Earth's cycles. When we open up to the possibility of our wisdom coming to us in other ways, we make space for a deeper connection to the Spirit World and ourselves.

Our relationship with the Moon is one such deep connection. As with every relationship we have with Creation, we believe that the Moon carries a Spirit. The Moon is part of our Kin, our family. Some even say it is our first family, so we have honored this relationship with the Moon and called her Grandmother. In this book, I will be using a gendered name for the Moon as my connection with Grandmother energy is deeply rooted. However I want to be sensitive to gendering aspects of Creation, and you will notice that I use nonbinary terms, "they/them," as much as possible. I hope that my intention to be inclusive is felt in my language choices.

Connection to the Moon is accessible to everyone. As an Indigenous person, the Full Moon has traditionally been a time to gather in a circle and share in Ceremony. In Anishinaabe teachings, our calendar is based on the 13 lunar cycles of a year. Not every year has 13 Full Moons, but the Moon orbits the Earth 13 times each year. The name of each Moon reflects the optimal times for planting seeds, gathering, and harvesting Plant Medicines and foods, or hunting for wild game. Different Nations had different stories, wisdom, teachings, and names for each of the Moons, depending on the climate, seasonal changes, Animal behavior, and the Land's teachings.

The 13 Moon names that I will be offering as a framework for this book are the Moons that have been shared through different Anishinaabe teachers. They are written in *Kinoomaadiewinan Anishinabek Bimaadinzinwin: Book Two* by Arlene Berry. The names and teachings of these 13 Moons have been used in my Ceremonies and circles. The wisdom I share at the beginning of each chapter encompasses the traditional teaching blended with my own knowing. This wisdom has flowed forward from facilitating hundreds of Moon circles. We must honor where our teachings are passed down from, and I am grateful for how these Moon teachings have supported me each month of my life.

The stories and legends that are shared at the beginning of each chapter are a co-creation between myself and Spirit. The teachings are rooted in Anishinaabe traditions and are here for you to experience so that you may feel the remembering of your innate wisdom, ancestry, and healing ways. You have everything you need to energetically access healing information from your body, mind, and Spirit.

New age and wellness communities co-opt Indigenous teachings and Medicine wisdom that is not theirs to take. Extraction in this way continues to cause harm to Indigenous communities. When people in a powerful and privileged position outside of a culture use those teachings for profit, it creates further oppression, marginalization, and pain. This book intends to offer teachings from my Anishinaabe tradition as a bridge or portal to find your Medicine ways. These teachings are not offered up to be taken or stolen but instead to be used as an invitation to awaken, catalyze, and illuminate all that is rooted within your blood, bones, and cells. Through each chapter, your intuition, inner guidance, and wisdom are most welcome. With me as your Guide, we will walk together, and you will rise into the magnetic Medicine keeper that you have always been, with wisdom rooted in your own lineage and ancestry.

Healing is a daily journey, one that calls us to a higher consciousness, acknowledgment, and personal responsibility. Healing is not always easy. A dedication to a healing path often means that we need to walk through many of our shadow parts, acknowledge our pain, and allow ourselves to see what needs to be seen. Through our journey together, you will be walking this path in a good way, *Mino-bimaadiziwin*. This may mean different things for different people. For me, walking in a "good" way means that I'm listening to my Ancestors' guidance and moving toward the Vision that Creator had for me. Similarly, Elders speak of walking the Red Road where we connect to our own Spirit and the guidance of the Spirit World. We take responsibility for our actions and speak the truth from our hearts. We will make mistakes along the way, of course, but we intend to come back to a place of introspection, compassion, and balance. I am inviting you into this space where you may go as deep as you desire to go. There is no right or wrong. There is only your way.

Over the past two decades, I have sat in circle with many souls longing to walk in this way. They desire a deeper connection to the elements of the Earth and their sacred spirituality. As we open our time together, I would love to invoke a devotional container space for you, my dear reader. If you have ever felt disconnected from your purpose, ancestry, and power, I see you. If you are longing to invite in the Medicine teachings of your Ancestors, I hear you. If you are looking for ways to invite more synchronicity, magic, and mystery into your life, I welcome you. I am here to meet you with the beauty of my Ancestors and the grace of my heart.

SACRED CIRCLE VISUALIZATION

Take a moment to tune in to your breath—feel it moving through your whole being. Feel the Earth energy beneath your feet. Envision yourself as a bright and sparkling Spirit being who can envision, sense, hear, and know deeply. Tune in to the energy of the left side of your body; you feel warmth, and a beautiful circle of beings begins to form. The same thing happens to your right. See the souls all gathering in a circle for this living, breathing manifestation of possibility. We intend for a rooted, safe, brave, and illuminated container to be made here and now. In the center, we light a bright fire for transmutation. We feel the Earth solid beneath us, holding and cradling our system. Above us are the Stars, Moon, and Sun, reminding us of the galaxies of spaciousness, and all around us, we call forward the Plant, Stone, Ancestors, and Animal Beings to hold this sacred container with us. We are now activated and ready to move through our journey with protection and amplified connection.

How to Journey through This Book

This book is based on the 13 Moon cycles in chronological order, at the start of the Gregorian calendar. Each Moon cycle has an accompanying Animal Spirit Medicine that will journey with us through that month. Because the Moon names and teachings are deeply aligned with the changes of the Earth, Seasons, and the Land, depending on where you are reading this, the Moon and the Month it occurs in, may not completely correlate with what is happening on the Lands where you live. These Moons are named based on the cyclical nature of my home territory, near the Georgian Bay in Ontario, Canada.

Each chapter starts with storytelling. When I was a little girl, my mother would read stories to me from *Tales of Nokomis,* a book by Patronella Johnston. It informed my understanding of our relationship with the natural world. The Animals, Trees, and Plants were filled with profound wisdom as they spoke and shared lessons—they are the storytellers. In this book, each chapter starts with a teaching that connects us to that particular Moon. We all can hear what our Earth Kin speak and share, and my intention for these legends is to help us all remember that we, too, can commune with the Land if we quiet our minds and listen with our hearts.

As mentioned, each chapter has an Animal Spirit woven through. At this time there are many Indigenous folks who believe that non-Indigenous folks cannot use Animal Medicine. As Indigenous people, we are not a monolith, and while I understand where this belief comes from, in my experience, Animal Medicine has been used by non-Indigenous people in respectful, reverent ways, and so I share it, trusting that you will use it with care. It's important to note that Animal Spirits are our Kin, siblings, protectors, guardians, and allies. They are sacred. I share this Medicine with you, hoping that you, too, will treat them this way. It is harmful to use our sacred relationship as a joke or reduce it to a meme (like, "My BFF is my Spirit Animal"). That takes us away from the depth of connection and sacredness that we are being called to when working with these Guides.

Throughout the chapter, you will find reflection questions. I have found that approaching our spiritual practice with curiosity and wondering are brilliant ways to stay connected to awe. I will remain a student forever and, as I walk toward Elderhood, I love to go deeper into my own Medicine through these types of reflections. Journal prompts are a powerful way to crack open deeper wisdom; if you are called, please have your journal ready so that you can write down everything that comes forward for you. Your Medicine, dear Wisdom Keeper, is waiting to be birthed through these words.

The journeys that accompany each chapter are channeled from my Ancestors. Their words are activated with divine healing energy that helps to clear and purify the past so that reconnection is possible. Each journey is a portal to further your soul growth and connection to the Spirit

World. As you read through, notice what sensations, visions, or memories come forward for you. The information might not come right away. Be open to the possibility of knowledge, wisdom, and remembering coming through your dreams, synchronicities, and other happenings in the days to come. These Medicine journeys are infused with intentions for your remembering and reclamation; use them as such.

Dreaming, envisioning, and imagining are all powerful ways to connect to the Spirit World. Much of the work I've done as a Medicine Person in this lifetime has occurred in these invisible realms. There is potency in the unseen. I would love to begin our time together by creating an energetic Sacred Space. When we create an intentional container to do our sacred work, the results are amplified and intensified. The blessings of that work are shared with those we serve: our communities, our Ancestors, and our descendants.

SACRED SPACE ENERGY ACTIVATION

When we intentionally set up our Sacred Space, we amplify our healing. Imagine thousands of folks reading these words and energetically creating containers for transformation. It's a powerful vision.

Feel into your body and begin to breathe. Allow this breath to move to the soles of your feet. They feel warm as you feel into the Land that you are occupying. Light blasts out of your heart, creating a container of love. This container is here to hold your healing work and evolution. Mother Earth shakes beneath you, and all of Creation leans in to assist you in creating this most Sacred Space.

The Trees offer you their trunks and roots to anchor this container.

The Plants offer you their Medicines and scents to help nourish this container.

The Waters of the Earth offer you their cleansing to help purify this container.

The Stones offer you their ancient wisdom to help this container evolve.

The Animals offer you their unique Medicines for when you have forgotten who you are.

The Fire offers you transmutation for when things need to be released.

The Ancestors offer you the vision they have dreamed for you.

The Moon, the Stars, the Sun, the Galaxies, and all the other beings step forward with their light, and they pulse it through this container.

Breathe. Allow. Invite. You are worthy of being held in this way.

This space is now set up for you to do your reflection and journeying work. The more we engage with the presence of our energetic Sacred Space, the more potent it becomes. You can access it any time you feel tired or need a recharge. This is your Medicine space.

Let's get started.

CHAPTER 1

WAYESHKAD IN THE BEGINNING

Our Creation stories bring us home to who we are. We call our Land Turtle Island, for we hold deep reverence for Turtle Medicine and its reminders of how to walk in right relationship with all beings. Turtle holds all of the 13 Moons on its back, the wisdom of the Sky reflected through its body. When we hold both the Earth and Sky as sacred, we remember that we, too, are part of this wholeness and all of Creation supports our path here.

MEDICINE LEGEND: HOW TURTLE ISLAND CAME TO BE

A long time ago, love, cooperation, and reciprocal relationships between all beings filled the Earth. All was well until the People started to argue over resources. Greed, jealousy, and envy took over the Earth, and fighting between the Nations began. Creator watched as their vision for the Earth was destroyed. They decided that something must be done to bring things back into balance. Water has incredible cleansing powers, and Creator felt that its Medicine could help renew, purify, and bring peace back to all of Creation. Water flooded the Earth, and the only ones who survived were some of the swimmers and winged ones. They gathered together and came up with the idea that if they could retrieve just one piece of the Earth, they could bring life back to the Land.

Loon, the amazing diver, volunteered to try first. They were confident that they would be able to get a piece of the Earth with ease. They dove down while all the others watched with hope. Loon took quite a while coming back up to the surface, and when they did, they shook their head. They could not get a piece of the Land. One by one, the swimmers tried—Perch, Otter, Beaver, and Trout—but none of them could retrieve the piece that they needed. Muskrat had been watching and observing all of the animals and softly said, "May I try?" All the other animals looked at Muskrat and laughed. "You are not a good enough swimmer, Muskrat—what do you know about deep diving? All you do is sit in the Water. This is too dangerous for you!"

Muskrat gently met the eyes of their Animal Kin and asked them again if they could try. Turtle's voice flowed through the Waters, reminding the Animals that this type of behavior is what got them here in the first place. Chastened, the Animals told Muskrat that they could try. It turned out that Muskrat was a great swimmer and was able to plunge deep into the Waters. The Animals waited with anticipation. Finally, after what seemed to be a long time, Muskrat rose through the Water holding a piece of the Earth in their claw. Having been under the Water so long, Muskrat was drained and gasping.

Turtle swam over to Muskrat and said they would carry this piece of Earth on their shell and back. Muskrat placed the piece of Earth on Turtle's back, and they realized how tired they were from their great journey. Sadly, Muskrat died and made their way to the Spirit World. As they returned to their place in the Stars, their Animal Kin said prayers of gratitude for saving the Earth.

The essence of gratitude began to grow and the Winged Ones flew to Turtle's shell to help birth the Earth back into being. They flapped their wings, and the winds from all the sacred directions began to stir up and activate the spread of the Soil. It began to take up more and more space, reaching out far and wide. Beauty, abundance, and life came back to the Earth, and this is the Land we now stand on and call Turtle Island.

This story has been passed down to me through my communication with Elders.

Animal Spirit: *Miskwaadesi* (Turtle)

The Animal Spirit that starts this book is the Turtle, or as they are known in Anishiinabemowin, *Miskwaadesi.* Turtle Medicine helps us to stay grounded, when we feel unsteady or out of alignment. It brings us back to our own roots and bodies. Turtle carries ancient wisdom and reminds us that we must move through all seasons and cycles to gain the insight we need on this path. This Animal reminds us to be intentional with our journey on the Earth; each step matters, as our presence and actions impact all of Creation. When we are feeling overwhelmed or agitated, Turtle steadies us and helps balance our nervous system. When we walk with Turtle, we feel peace and security, moving through the cycles of life with more ease and connection.

Turtle Message

- We are all Creators.
- Return to your roots of divinity.
- All cycles and seasons are Medicine.
- Slow Medicine matters.

YOUR ORIGINAL INSTRUCTIONS

It has been said that we are Star beings in human form. We have journeyed from the Cosmos and landed here, earthbound in a body, and given unique instructions on how to spend our time on this planet. After facilitating healing for many people and working with their energy bodies, this feels true to me. Returning to our original instructions and remembering our divine essence is an essential part of our human journey. These original instructions were gifted to us from Creator and speak to how we will move in our fullest presence and power. Our truest nature is divine, made of Stardust and clear channels of truth and beauty. I know that returning to this vision is much easier said than done, but perhaps, like me, you've had glimpses of how this feels.

I've felt this when I am rooted in my Medicine Work, eyes closed, journeying with spiritual energies and my Ancestors. I've felt this when I walk in nature and look at Grandfather Sun shining through the trees. I've felt this when I dance or sing or play the piano. These times in my life help me return to my original instructions, and I know that these moments are available to you, too; you just need to be curious and open to receiving the remembering.

> **Medicine Reflection:** What is your Creation story? What parts have you forgotten that you need to remember?

MEDICINE JOURNEY:
Remembering Your Original Instructions

Find a comfortable place to sit or lie down and breathe deeply. Set your intention to travel back in time to recover your original instructions. Close your eyes and envision a candle flame in front of you. Feel yourself moving into the flame; it's warm and not too hot. As you move through this flame, you travel through your lifetime, each stage, age, and cycle. Move back in time to your birth, into the Womb, and move then beyond, back to the Stars, to the time you were a spark of divine light. In your vision, you are energy and light, and you meet with Creator/Universal/Love energy. You ask to remember your original instructions.

In this space, there are no conditions on your worth; there is only love. Your Creation story gets downloaded into your mind, body, and Spirit. Take a moment to breathe in this remembering. Receive it and let it take up space. You might see it as a vision, sense it as an understanding, hear it as a story, or know it in some way. If you have a hard time remembering, trust that with every moment that lights up your heart, you are coming home to who you are. You are divine perfection. Creator makes no mistakes.

When you feel complete, begin to move forward in time, soaring back as light, creating your Creation story as you move back into your physical form, through your mother's womb space, and into your human body. As you see yourself moving through every stage and every age, walk the energy of who you are into being. It strengthens with every step. Feel your Creation story embodied as you feel the energy flooding you from head to toe. Wiggle your toes to allow it to flow and gently breathe yourself back into this space and time.

You are the Medicine.

1. *Mnido Giizis* –
   Spirit Moon

2. *Mkwa Giizis* –
   Bear Moon

3. *Ziisbaakdoke Giizis* –
   Sugar Moon

4. *Namebine Giizis* –
   Suckerfish Moon

5. *Waawaaskone Giizis* –
   Flower Moon

6. *Ode'miin Giizis* –
   Strawberry Moon

7. *Mskomini Giizis* –
   Raspberry Moon

8. *Datkaagmiin Giizis* –
   Blackberry Moon

9. *Mdaamiin Giizis* –
   Corn Moon

10. *Biinaakwe Giizis* –
    Falling Leaves Moon

11. *Mshkawji Giizis* –
    Freezing Moon

12. *Mnidoons Giizisoonhg*
    – Little Spirit Moon

13. *Mnidoons Giizis* –
    Big Spirit Moon

13 MOONS

If you look at a turtle's back, you will see that the patterning represents something beautiful and synchronistic with the pattern of the lunar calendar. There are 13 Moon phases within our 12-month calendar year—from January to December. The extra Moon occurs about every 2.7 years, so depending on which year you are reading this, there may or may not be 13 Full Moons; however, the Moon goes through her cycle 13 times. When you look at a turtle shell, the circle of markings that surround the edge of the shell will add up to 28. The number 28 is equivalent to the number of days from one Full Moon to the next. The inner circle of the shell has 13 markings, which represent each one of the Moon phases of our lunar calendar. This connection between the turtle shell and the Moon is a prime example of how intricate and connected all of Creation is. This image will guide us through our time together as we journey through each month. Turtle will be holding us, rooting us, and helping us remember our own Creation stories. It's time to tune in to your own sacred pulse and call forward the rhythm of your Ancestors.

MEDICINE JOURNEY
13 Moon Activation with Turtle

Find a comfortable space to sit or lie down. Take a breath into your belly and feel it rise and fall. Envision your breath moving all the way down to the base of your spine, feeling an expansion and warmth of energy moving up and down the length of your spine. You see or sense Turtle appearing in front of you. They are a wise and ancient being, and as you place your hands on their shell, you feel yourself steadying. Welcome this energy into your body with inhalation and feel a strong and steady Turtle shell appear on your back. This calms your nervous system, and your spine will tingle with the sensation of this shell activating.

It moves down your spine from top to bottom. Feel into the security and stability that this brings you. You can come back to this sensation at any time. Look up into the Sky and see Grandmother Moon radiating in the darkness. She is in her fullness, a large circle in the darkness. Radiant light streams into the top of your head and down your Turtle shell spine, activating your connection to both Earth and Sky. On your back, you now carry the wisdom of the 13 Moons. The Medicines and teachings are ready to be activated in your life. When you feel disconnected or out of sorts, remember the stable shell on your back. You can lean into this any time you need to.

MOON MAGIC

When I was a little girl, I remember feeling delighted when I would ride in the car at night and look out at the Moon. It seemed like she was following me. I remember the Moons that appeared pink in the Sky and large harvest Moons that awed me. I would dream of what it would be like to fly there and explore. My mother would always point out the Moon and share her love for its magnificence. Her child-like joy of the natural world imparted deep wisdom about the beauty of this great Earth.

If you are reading this book, I'm sure that you can relate to my love of the Moon. Grandmother Moon has been with you since the day you were a spark in your Mother's Womb. She has been reminding you to listen to your inner pulse and rhythm. The gravitational pull of the Moon impacts the Water of the Earth. You, too, are made of Water, and she beckons you to rise and fall in the same way. Indigenous people have always listened to these cycles and honored their sacred relationship with these parts of Creation. The Moon is our Elder, our Grandmother, our Guide.

Sadly, our modern-day attachment to technology has led many people to disconnect from the Medicine that the Earth can gift us. We have forgotten how to listen to the sacred pulse that runs through our blood from our Ancestors. We have forgotten that there are cycles and seasons to everything. We have favored hustle over rest, achievement over listening to our natural cycles. And every night, the Moon rises, as if to say, "Come back to the rhythm of your own body, mind, and Spirit." She is here to inform us always.

Medicine Reflection: What's your current relationship with the Moon and her cycles? How does her Medicine teach you?

As an Indigenous person who has a physical womb and experiences menses, the Moon is especially close to me. Grandmother Moon is said to watch over the Earth's Waters, which means that her power impacts my own Sacred Waters. She governs my cycle, and my Moon time (menses) is a potent time. Traditionally, it is said that when one experiences their Moon time, that they are closer to Creator. We honor the great power that we hold during our menses, and our teachings ask us to rest, cleanse, and renew. During this time, we are not supposed to work with Medicines or certain ceremonial items. Some even believe we should not prepare food. It is a sacred time for introspection, and it is also a time when we are deeply intuitive.

If we go back to our Creation story, we will remember that Water was offered to the Earth through a flood, and then new life came to be. Water is the first Medicine gifted to us. We swim in the Waters of our mother's Womb, receiving the sacred space that we need in which to grow. Whether or not we choose to have children, any person with a physical womb space carries this miraculous power. People with wombs hold this sacred connection to all of Creation, the power to create new life. In Indigenous societies, this is a power that is honored and upheld by all people. Creator chooses us to be the divine portal that connects the Spirit to the physical. Of course, this is not a path that everyone desires, which is honored.

Years before my first menses, I remember my mother buying me books about my body and the changes and transitions it would go through. I remember diving in deep, excited for these changes to happen to me. The teachings I received were that this was a sacred and beautiful time and that this transition should be celebrated. My mother shared these Creation teachings with me and modeled the power we have always held in our communities. As a result, I have always honored my menses as a time of beauty, fascinated by the wonder and miracle of my body. I will cherish every cycle that I continue to move through, knowing that when this part of my life ends, my energy will then be preserved for my role as an Elder.

Through patriarchal oppression and marginalization of women, we have lost our sacred connection to this time. Women have carried shame and disconnection around their menses, seeing it as a nuisance, something that brings them pain, or something to hide. I have always been curious about what might look different in our world if we reclaimed the power of our Moon time. What would happen if we took this time each month to rest deeply, dream well, and access our intuitive knowing? Imagine that we asked our family, friends, and loved ones for the spaciousness that we need, and they respected the potency of our Medicine at this time. I hold a vision in my heart that we will all return to the sacred, miraculous creators that we are by remembering these teachings and our connection to the Moon. You are Earth; the rhythm of your Ancestors moves through your sacred pulse with every season and cycle. Connected and rooted to both Soil and the Stars, your wisdom is innate.

Medicine Reflection: What is your connection with the Moon? Do you honor the cyclical Medicine within?

Turtle Medicine Invocation

Dearest Turtle, I invite you in to help me remember my connection to all of Creation. Root me to the Earth and help me see my reflection in the light of the Moon. As you impart your Medicine into my life, I am open to receiving your wisdom—that your slow pulse can offer stability. Your pace is divine. When I find myself rushing, help me to remember the importance of measured movement.

Moon Medicine Affirmation

Dearest Grandmother Moon, I invite you into my body, mind, and Spirit. May your Medicine fill me up with the cycle that I am most aligned with at this time. I am committed to listening to how you pull on my sacred Waters, my blood, my fluids. With your Medicine, I settle into the greater knowing that whatever cycle I may be in is perfect for me. Through your teachings, I remember that without darkness, there cannot be light. I am the Medicine.

CHAPTER 2

MNIDO GIIZIS SPIRIT MOON

Our first Moon of Creation occurs in January, where the landscape is covered with snow. It is connected to the brilliance of the Northern Lights. It is a time to be silent and honor the quiet. Silence helps us to reflect. Reflection helps us to clarify what is not ours to carry. In these moments, we make more room for our truest essence to shine. Just like the Northern Lights, we, too, hold magnificence, beauty, and wonder. We are a vital part of Creation, and this Moon asks us to awaken to that truth.

MOON LEGEND: HOW THE NORTHERN LIGHTS CAME TO BE

In the beginning, Creator envisioned Celestial energies into being: the Sun, the Moon, the Stars, and the Planets. The day would move into the night, and the Celestial beings would take their turns illuminating the Sky. All of Creation would watch in awe as the Sun set over the horizon and left behind a watercolor display of beauty. This was a gift from the Sun and one that was deeply valued by all of the beings on the Earth.

The Moon, Stars, and Planets watched the beauty the Sun would offer, and they started to feel a bit jealous and overlooked. "We want something in our night Sky that looks like that! It's not fair that the Sun gets all the beauty," they pouted. But day after day, the Sun continued to create new skies at sunset, changing the colors, each day more lovely than the last.

The other Celestial beings became incensed. They could not handle how much attention the Sun was getting. They gossiped with each other and made fun of the Sun. "Who does Sun think they are?" they said. "Those on the Earth rarely see our colors," complained the Planets. Together, they devised a plan to steal the colors once the Sun went down. "Maybe we could steal the colors and have them all for ourselves," said the Stars. "Brilliant," said the Moon, "and because I am a shapeshifter, I will be the best at stealing. The rest of you can distract the other beings of Creation so they don't see me."

As the Celestial beings schemed and planned, the Great Thunderbird flew nearby, listening, for they often visited the Upper World. Thunderbird carried great responsibility to help all beings maintain their integrity. They were not happy with what they heard and decided to find a way to intercept this plan. The next day at sundown, Thunderbird saw the Stars, the Moon, and the Planets get into place to steal the colors of the sunset. Thunderbird called up their incredibly potent Medicine, flapped their wings, and expanded until they took up much of the Sky, creating darkness. The Celestial beings began to shake. "What's happening?" they all said, confused and afraid.

Thunderbird roared. "I saw what you were going to do, dear Stars, Moon, and Planets. Your jealousy causes great harm. It's time to see yourself in your truest nature. Do you not know how glorious you are when you illuminate the dark Sky? Spin in your own way? Dance with your own light? You are pure magic and grace."

The Celestial beings witnessed their unique, sparkling beauty in the darkness Thunderbird had created and felt ashamed. "In our jealously of the Sun, we have forgotten our unique radiance. We are deeply sorry," they said.

They went before the Sun and asked for their forgiveness with humble and open hearts. The Sun forgave their Kin, and Thunderbird was pleased with the healing that resulted. Thunderbird stood before all of the Celestial beings and said: "Beauty comes in all forms. We must honor the differences in our gifts and abilities. As a reminder of this, I am going to offer you a gift."

They all watched as Thunderbird flew up into the Sky with one huge flap of their wings, a loud boom followed. A flash of lightning darted through the Night Sky, and all of a sudden, there was an explosion of beautiful colors dancing everywhere. All the beings of the Earth were in awe and gratitude filled their hearts.

"These are the Northern Lights," said Thunderbird. "When you see them dancing in the Sky, may they always remind you that you don't have to put others down in order to rise. Your beauty is breathtaking. May you always see and honor this within yourself."

Animal Spirit: *Animikii Binesi* (Thunderbird)

The Animal Spirit that best represents the first Moon is Thunderbird, or as they are known in Anishiinabemowin,

Animikii Binesi. Thunderbird has vital Medicine that helps us walk in integrity with who we are. Thunderbird moves through this Moon phase to teach us that we are brought into alignment when we stand tall in our gifts and claim our space in Creation. We must see the power that we all hold as unique beings, and hold that purpose here as we journey upon this Earth. We often get off track from our original purpose when we compare ourselves to others and envy what others have. Of course, this is all part of the human experience, and Thunderbird is here to reflect our power to us. The more we can walk aligned with our Original Instruction, staying in the lane that Creator envisioned for our life, the more we can shine in our authentic light. Of course, it takes daily practice to continuously align ourselves with our energy and see that what we have to offer the world is of great value.

Thunderbird Message

- You have a vital place in the community; your authentic light is needed.

- When comparison or jealousy rises, use it for inspiration.

- Be honest about your strengths. It's okay not to excel at everything in life. The most important thing is that you commit to growth.

- You hold the strength of thunder in your heart and the brilliance of lightning in your belly. It's time to see yourself in truth.

I WANT WHAT YOU HAVE

When I was in homeopathy school, I had this friend who was an incredibly gifted Healer. In my first session with her, the beauty of her healing studio took my breath away. She had hundreds of books lining the walls, crystals in every corner, and shelves of remedies all organized perfectly. Her healing bed looked so cozy, and she had all of these tools to assist her in her work. I was in awe.

Every time I would see her, I would feel a slight pang—wishing that someday, in some way, I, too, would have a sacred space to call my own, where I could offer healing to those who needed it. She seemed so well put together, professional, and organized. I shared this dream with her one day, saying that I admired what she had created for her life. "You will have this, too, Asha. I see it." I tucked that sentiment into my heart and continued in my studies.

Years later, I was in my own cozy healing space and I saw it: the crystals, the books, the remedies, and the healing tools. I flashed back to that conversation and understood the mirror of inspiration that Healer friend had been for me. At that time, I did not know that I would be an energetic Healer or use my gifts in that way. She reflected back a part of me that I hadn't yet uncovered. I knew that she was in my life for a reason, and it was to show me what was possible. I learned to look at life in that way, see these mirrors as future blessings, and turn my envy into possibility.

JOURNEY IN YOUR OWN MOCCASINS

How many times have you looked at someone else's path and thought it looked better than yours? Have you ever wished that you were blessed by the same circumstances as another? I know I have, and I have learned not to feel ashamed of this because it's human nature. We compare and contrast in order to find our way; it's part of our evolution and growth. These feelings have been amplified with the introduction of social media. We must remember that what we see there is only a tiny slice of someone's life. We do ourselves a disservice when that is all that we are looking at, peering into a highly curated space. After sitting with thousands of students, I can tell you this truth: Nobody's life is perfect. We have all been gifted with our own Creation story, our soul called to different missions. One mission is not better or worse than another. Spirit Moon reminds us that when we can cradle our Medicine Journey and path with reverence; we can see that the only moccasins we are meant to move in are our own. If I see someone journeying in a way that inspires me or lights me up, I begin to lean into the possibility that I, too, can have those things. I have learned to see that my desires are being blessed by the way they show up in the world. I cannot walk in the exact same way, but I can call similar blessings to me.

> **Medicine Reflection:** Whose life have you compared to yours? Which aspects do you desire for yourself?

YOUR AUTHENTIC PRESENCE

There are billions of people upon this planet and each holds a different tone of soul expression. The resonance of your being is unique to you. I've played the piano for many years, so I liken this to a particular cord, harmonic sound, or energetic cadence. Our world will always tell us that we are not enough as we are. External programming, societal expectations, and collective noise will try to distract us from our true nature. When we can attune ourselves to our frequency, own it, and move it into the world, we find peace in our path and can align in our divinity.

For the 15 years I had a private practice as a Healer, there was a prayer that I would say before each person would enter my space: *Dear Creator, may I honor, see, and hold space for this soul and their most authentic presence.* My intention with each patient was to envision them as whole in the state they came to see me in. I had been on my own journey of healing long enough to know that it wasn't helpful to be told over and over again how broken I was. I knew that the most significant healing gift I could offer someone was to see them in their fullness.

Through my work with these clients—energy work, Ceremony, and homeopathy—I would hold the vision and energetic frequency that I saw through my eyes, heart, and Spirit. I remember being able to see this from a very young age. Perhaps it was part of the Medicine that came into this life with me. What they perceived as their shadow—the "mistakes" they made or "flaws" they carried—I held tenderly, and met with compassion. In my vision, I would hold their authentic presence firm and rooted, an imprinted prayer for their remembering. Part of my "job" was to hold that vibration of their authentic presence and somehow reflect it in our time together. Seeing yourself in your truth takes daily practice, and sometimes we all need reminders. Each day, we can intentionally center our true nature. The distractions and demands of everyday life too often sway us from coming home to ourselves. As with anything, practice creates new pathways that become second nature if experienced time and time again. The energy of Spirit Moon helps us to root this in and shine as we are.

Four Ways to Connect to Your Authentic Presence

1. *Display artwork or images that speak to your soul.*

   There are two Indigenous artists that I love—Betty Albert and Maxine Noel—and their paintings are all around my home. The images depict women standing with grace, flow, and connection. Many of the pictures contain the Moon or Animals. They speak to me because they reflect an aspect of my authentic self. By placing them around my home, they surround me as mirrors of my soul expression.

2. *Look at a picture of your child self.*

   Take a moment and stare into your own eyes and ask to see your unique presence. When your child self was rooted in their joy and freedom, what shined out from their heart?

3. *Take a journey to reclaim and root into your authentic presence.*

   After you take a journey—like the one below—connect to the images, vibrations, and sensations of your presence.

4. *Bring your experience into a morning practice.*

   Take a few moments upon waking to call on your unique presence before you get out of bed. When you stand up, feel yourself "stepping in" or "zipping yourself up" into this aspect of yourself. One day, it will become second nature, and you will find yourself instantly aligned.

MEDICINE JOURNEY
Align Your Presence

Find a comfortable place to sit or lie down, and begin to breathe. We set the intention to call our most aligned presence forward. We ask for the Great Thunderbird to assist us in this journey today. They stand before you, look deeply into your heart, and send a blast of lightning to your arms, activating your ability to soar. They ask you to take a journey with them, and as they begin to rise into the Sky, you follow. You soar to the Stars, and there is one particular Star that calls to you. As you fly toward it, you feel a sense of familiarity. This Star carries the same resonance as your authentic presence. You stand before it, with your wings wide open. Thunderbird calls on a boom of Thunder Medicine, and you are blasted with light. As you absorb this healing, it reminds you of your divinity.

Breathe this in, allow it to flow through every cell and tissue of your being. Your authentic presence begins to pour out of your skin, and your whole energy is vibrating with your resonance. The Star now becomes a mirror, and you see yourself, radiant in your being.

Activate all your senses and ask yourself:
- How does your authentic presence sound?
- Do you carry a specific tone or vibration?
- What colors swirl around and through you?
- What are you wearing, and how do you appear?

This is who you are. It's time to claim your place in Creation. *And so, it is.* Thunderbird begins to guide you back, and you start to return to the Earth. Feel your feet returning to the Land, your wings changing back into arms, and your breath calling you back into your body. Bring your authentic presence back with you and feel it rooting into your body. *You are the Medicine.*

Fitting in is about assessing a situation and becoming who you need to be accepted. Belonging, on the other hand, doesn't require us to change who we are; it requires us to be who we are.

— BRENÉ BROWN, *Braving the Wilderness: The Quest for True Belonging and the Courage to Stand Alone*

IDENTITY

The word *Anishinaabe* has been said to mean "the Good Human." Elder and linguist Basil Johnston also translated it as "the Spontaneous Being." Basil was an old residential school friend of my Grandfather, and I remember him visiting and chatting in Anishiinabemowin at my Grandparents' kitchen table. The Spontaneous Being brings forward images of Starlight created from nothingness. I have always felt guided to live this way and return to this, remembering this image whenever I feel like I don't belong.

The feeling of not belonging is something that rises within all of us. It's a feeling that has been expressed to me hundreds of times by my clients, especially those of mixed blood. It's something I, too, have wrestled with, even though both of my parents are Anishinaabe. For those of us who have been colonized or impacted deeply by systems of oppression, this feeling of not belonging runs deep. We are told that we are not good enough as we are, so we try to assimilate into another way. Then we find out that those ways aren't aligned with the Medicine that echoes in our blood. We end up with one foot in one identity and one foot in the other, not quite knowing where we fit. As Indigenous people, we were fed racist stereotypes that told us that to be Native is to be dirty, poor, an alcoholic, a squaw, invisible. It doesn't seem safe to be who we are, so we run from that identity. But then, when we realize something is missing and come back home to embrace our truth, we don't feel like we fit into the spaces in community or Ceremony either. We don't know enough of our language. We don't know all the protocols for Ceremony. We feel shame at the hands of the colonizer. It's not our fault, yet we blame ourselves. And because of all this trauma, we weaponize these wounds and attack each other through lateral violence.

None of this is okay, and none of this will move us toward healing, yet we get stuck here. Maybe you can relate to this, or perhaps your belonging story is expressed differently. I dream that as we reclaim our whole selves, we can find belonging within. As we do this, we become secure, rooted, and can stand tall. Thunderbird energy helps us in this rising, and we can all do this, no matter our race, creed, or religion. I walk as Starlight created from nothingness, a proud Anishinaabe Kwe.

Medicine Reflection: What is your experience of belonging?

SEARCHING FOR A TEACHER

Even though I have journeyed with many teachers, for the longest time I was on a path to find the "perfect" Indigenous Elder who would guide me through this life. Traditionally, we would have Elders in community with us who would offer us teachings, support, and healing. Sadly, this is not as accessible anymore, as we don't live in communities in the same way. Many times I've felt that there was a missing piece to my path.

I would ask for Creator to bring me the one who would teach me all I needed to know. Different guides would come in and out of my life. One day, a Medicine Person I was working with gifted me a Pipe. As he laid it down in my hands, I realized my truth: I didn't need an object to communicate with Spirit. I had already been doing it for my whole life. My Pipe is sacred and so are my innate and developed Medicines. Wisdom has always emerged through my life experiences. The one "perfect" teacher was me. Yes, I could invite in other guides, but my path was meant to have a diverse set of teachers and way-showers, myself included. An Elder shared with me to keep my heart open, as my teachers will not always be Indigenous. I have taken this wisdom to heart, and I open my mind to all who can teach me, knowing that my learning will continue until my last breath.

Taking Up Space

Our identities often impact our ability to take up space. I recognize that I carry privilege as a cisgender, straight, thin, able-bodied human who manages a chronic illness relatively well. I also hold the identity as an Indigenous person who lives on the Land stolen from her Ancestors. Because the colonizer took the Land and oppressed my people, it has been a challenge to feel entitled to take up space here, even though I am one of the original people of this Land. When you live in a body that carries privilege in any way, you will feel more entitled to take up all of the space you need. The world has made it safe for you to do so. In a world where the messaging is that Indigenous folks are invisible and forgotten, I have journeyed to claim my right to be seen, heard, and held here on Turtle Island. This is essential work for me. Through my healing, I slowly feel more comfortable standing here with pride and taking up the space I deserve. I am reminded that my taking up space will not take away from anyone else; instead, as I reclaim what belongs to me, I help repair the past and hold a vision for a healed future. We can look to Spirit Moon to guide us back to what it feels like to live with a healthy and balanced sense of entitlement. If you, too, have challenges taking up space, please know that it's not something to be ashamed of. It's most likely a product of living in the systems we live in, and those systems need to change.

Medicine Reflection: Do you feel comfortable taking up space? Why or why not?

It's Not Your Nature

Every month for the past three years, I have met with my incredible therapist who has gifted me with much wisdom. There was a time where I was personally under a lot of stress with concerns around how I walk as an activist in the world. I felt a lot of pressure to show up in ways that others were, even though it didn't feel authentic to me. One day I received a message in my inbox. "Why aren't you sharing about these Indigenous issues in this way? I expected more from you! Unfollowing!" I was crushed. I had already been comparing myself and feeling like my way of activism wasn't enough. I took this to my appointment and was ready to learn how to show up as a different voice in another way—a way that would somehow satisfy these expectations of what an Indigenous voice should be.

I met with my therapist and told him that I was ready to become louder, more assertive, feistier. More of something that I wasn't being. He listened with grace, as he always does, and shared this simple wisdom with me: "It's simply not your nature, Asha."

I took a deep breath, and peace flowed over me. In an instant, the doubting stopped as my inner critic was met with compassion.

"What kind of activist do you want to be?' he asked.

"A Peaceful Warrior," I exclaimed. "I want to put down my sword and exist differently."

"That sounds closer to your true nature," he said.

A few days after this meeting, I met with one of my business besties, Leslie Tagorda from New Moon Creative, and she shared her astrological insights with me. "Your path on this Earth is to be the Peaceful Warrior," she said. "It's right here, in your chart." I must have gasped out loud. Confirmation, right from the Stars! The path was always there, and I was already walking it. All I needed was to remember. I share this story because no matter where you might be on your personal development journey, we all experience doubt and insecurity. We can all forget that our presence is so much more than enough. I'm always eternally grateful for these confirmatory signs from the Universe that guide me back to me. They often show up through my friends, my colleagues, my helpers, my Guides. Everyone is a teacher and a beautiful mirror for me to remember.

> **Medicine Reflection:** Have you ever tried to be something that does not align with the truth of who you are? How does that feel?

Thunderbird Medicine Invocation

Dearest Thunderbird, I invite you to remind me of my wings, my essence, my vibrational imprint on this world. Remind me that just like the Northern Lights, I, too, carry beauty and radiance. I welcome in your Medicine, which reminds me to live in integrity with my own essence. If I find myself comparing my journey to that of others, help guide me back to my radiant presence. Your wings, Thunder Spirit, and lightning energy now fill my cells with inspiration. I trust that you will continue to guide me as I soar.

Mindo Giizis Moon Affirmation

I awaken to the truth of all that I am. My authentic presence is sacred; I see it, feel it, and know it. Each day I invoke it to come forward so that I may walk in true integrity with my nature. I am the Medicine.

○)))⟩ ⟩ ⟩●⟨ ⟨ ⟨⟨ ⟨⟨ ⟨○

CHAPTER 3

MKWA GIIZIS
BEAR MOON

Our second Moon of Creation is a time when we reflect on the Medicine of rest and integration. Just like the Bear who hibernates for many months, we, too, need seasons in which to slow down. It is said that this Moon in February brings heavy fog, a sign for the traditional Indigenous people that Bear cubs are born. We fall into the void with deep rest, where the Great Mystery can move through us in more extraordinary ways. With deep rest, miracles happen.

MOON LEGEND: WHY BEAR BEGAN TO HIBERNATE

When the Animals came to be, Creator gave each of them a particular Medicine that they would carry in the world. One by one, the Animals were dreamed into being by Creator, and one by one, their Medicine activated. Bear was one of the first in line. "Dear Creator, what is the gift that you bestow upon me?" Creator swirled beautiful energy around Bear and spoke the gift into the Universe. "You are a keeper of courage, dear Bear. Fierce in your boundaries, you stand rooted in your sovereignty. You are passionate about protecting those that you love and mirror the importance of standing your ground. Use your gifts wisely; we are grateful to have your Medicine upon the Earth."

Bear was elated with their Medicine gift. They felt strong and powerful and felt called to share their talents with everyone they met. When one of their Kin needed protection, Bear would appear to fight and serve. When one of their Kin needed help to speak up or try something new, Bear would appear to teach and inspire. Bear was being asked to do more and more each day, running from one problem to the next. Wolf lost their voice and their ability to snarl, so Bear stepped up and growled for them. Mountain Lion had too many babies to take care of, so Bear offered to carry some around for a while until they grew. All of Creation began to think that Bear had superpowers— whenever they needed help, Bear seemed to appear. Since Bear never complained or seemed tired, they just kept asking for support and help.

One day, Bear started to feel dizzy and ill, and they fell to the Earth in exhaustion. All of the Animals came running over, wondering what had happened. "Bear, what's wrong?" they cried. Bear couldn't speak, move, or open their eyes. They had run out of energy. The Animals, worried that Bear was dying, moved Bear into a nearby cave. They covered Bear with moss and Soil and flowers. Every day Owl checked on Bear and found that their temperature, heart rate, and breathing had dropped. Bear's eyes remained closed. The Animals came and went, offering prayers and gratitude for all that Bear had done for them.

One day, when the birds were chirping and the Sun brought longer days, Bear started to stretch and move. At first, the Animals thought they might be imagining things, but lo and behold, Bear finally opened their eyes.

They started to move slowly at first, and then they seemed to gain strength gradually. When Bear walked out of the cave, all of the Animals cheered. "Bear, we were so worried about you! We are sorry we asked you to do so much for us. We promise never to do that again."

"That's okay, dear Kin," said Bear. "It is my responsibility to manage my own energy. I know this now. From now on, I will be mindful of my capacity to help, and when I feel tired, I will listen to my body and rest. Because I offer so much, sometimes my rest will need to be longer. Perhaps it might span the whole time that the Earth Mother is blanketed in snow. But please know that I will be ready to serve in my place of Creation again when I reappear. I promise to listen to my body, retreat when needed, and trust that all will be taken care of in my absence." From that day forward, Bear listened to the wisdom of their body, which was attuned to the seasons. When food was scarce and the elements harsh, Bear knew it was time to conserve their energy and hibernate. When the conditions of the Earth were more favorable for survival, Bear would emerge again, ready to share their Medicine with all whom they love.

Animal Spirit: *Mkwa* (Bear)

The Animal Spirit that best represents the second Moon is the Bear, or as they are known in Anishiinabemowin, *Mkwa.* This Animal is an obvious choice, based on the name of this Moon, but it also speaks to the time of year that their cubs are born—which is usually in mid-January to mid-February. Bear moves through this Moon phase to teach us that the cycle of hibernation is necessary in order to integrate all other aspects of our lives. When we pause, there is deep magic that happens that we may not always see. The void, the quiet, the season of rest are vital to our wholeness. Without restoration and integration, we are incomplete. Productivity, striving, and material success are so deeply ingrained in our psyche. Our world teaches us to push harder, strive for more, and drive ourselves at the expense of our health and well-being. Bear reminds us of the power in slowing down. They remind us to stop so that we can listen to the wise call of our bodies. Our bodies, minds, and spirits can only hold so much. When our capacity is full, Bear encourages us to move into a cycle of rest as Medicine.

Bear Message

- You are worthy of rest.
- Listen to the messages from your body.
- Magic is birthed from the void.
- The Great Mystery moves through us, even when it appears that nothing is happening.

"IF I REST, I WILL DIE."

When I was 17, I was diagnosed with an autoimmune condition called SLE or lupus. It is a chronic condition in which the immune system attacks your own tissues and organs, mistaking them for invaders. I remember the day that I was diagnosed; I felt highly anxious. I was worried I would die early, not have children, or be in pain every day for the rest of my life. It was shocking as a teenager to receive this news, and I spent a lot of time worrying about my health.

It wasn't until I was in university that the severe symptoms began to show up, and I noticed that I seemed to need more rest than my friends did. I remember coming home and napping every day at 3 p.m. I wondered why I was so tired and what was wrong with me. I started to hide the fact that I needed this extra rest and eventually shamed myself so much that I just stopped taking the rest my body cried out for and pushed through my days.

I tried to live like I saw everyone else living. I never offered myself the compassion to think that maybe, since I was dealing with a chronic illness, I needed to take better care of myself or give myself a break every so often. I just continued to push through. This became a habit: forcing myself through my pain, ignoring the fatigue, expecting so much of myself. My inner oppressor was always telling me to hustle, even when I felt exhausted and overwhelmed.

When I didn't listen to my body, the nudges would get louder, eventually becoming symptoms, more extended flares, and illness. Our world teaches us to push harder, go for more, and drive ourselves at the expense of our health and well-being. This leads to burnout, chronic disease, and other disorders. Many of us lose the ability to make rest and play a priority, and if we continue in this way, our bodies will stop us. The wisdom of Bear Moon calls us back to the truth that it is not humanly possible to move through life without breaks. We are Earth, and we, too, must cycle through our seasons.

One day I was on a healing journey with a practitioner, and I asked my Spirit what the root of this issue was. I heard: *If I rest, I will die,* and tears streamed down my face. Flashes of Ancestral trauma moved through my awareness, and it felt like truth rooted in my bones. I remember recounting this story to my dear friend, and she asked: "What if you invited these words into your system instead? *If I rest, I will live."*

This statement has guided me ever since. Rest gives me life force; rest helps me integrate the cycles of expansion I move through; and rest opens me up to inspiration. I have learned that miracles touch my life through rest. It's been a constant growth edge for me to trust that rest is an integral part of my flow and Creation process. But each time I allow myself to deepen into rest as Medicine, I thrive.

> **Medicine Reflection:** How was rest modeled by your parents or family? What is your relationship to rest?

THE GIFT OF THE SACRED PAUSE

A number of years ago, I was at a Hay House "I Can Do It!" conference and Cheryl Richardson took the stage. She was sharing her new book at the time, *Waking Up in Winter*, and speaking about being present with what truly matters. She shared her own journey around hustling and achievement and how her inner world was calling her to get quiet. There was a profound moment about letting go, where Cheryl shared about "emptying her chalice," a metaphor for clearing away things that no longer served her. I remembered seeing this as a womb space in my mind's eye and could feel the potential of what could come from this spacious void.

Throughout the talk, I felt like she was speaking directly to my soul. She shared that her dear friend Debbie Ford had been on her deathbed and told Cheryl that at the end of her life, nothing Cheryl was currently focusing on would matter. Not the followers or the best-selling books. None of this mattered when you are about to die. She told Cheryl that all that truly mattered was living a life of presence. Presence. My soul wanted that.

At that time in my life, I was completely burnt out in my private practice. I was running from one healing circle to the next, seeing five or six people per day for deep healing work and parenting a three-year-old. I turned to my friend and whispered, "I need to do that! I need my version of Winter." The next day I looked at my calendar and moved all my patients to the next month. I took an entire month off from my practice, something that I never thought I would do. Something deeper was calling to me, a new season. I could not push any longer, and my soul was begging me to stop.

It was uncomfortable to stop. I worried about disappointing people, worried about how I would make money, and worried about becoming irrelevant. "What if I lose everything? What if everyone forgets about me? Who will I be?" I was deeply attached to the identity I had lived with for all these years. All of this discomfort rose to the surface, and I finally had some space to feel it. I remember taking that month off for more walks outside, more piano playing, more tea dates with friends, and even some naps. There were still many moments filled with doubt and fear, but also moments of peace and grace. At the end of my time, it became apparent that I have spent my entire lifetime equating my worth with how much I produce or achieve. This knowing was a gift, and it helped me to hold this pattern with compassion.

The following month, I had a gorgeous and unexpected surprise: a positive pregnancy test! We weren't trying for another child, as we had felt that our family was complete. Looking back, I can see that a part of me knew that I didn't have the capacity for another child with my busy practice and all the nurture and support I was holding for others. I needed to surrender and let go of what had felt safe to my system in order to co-create with Spirit. This experience and so many more are how I know that miracles come from the darkness. Just like the first spark of light, Creation stems from the void. Brand new bear cubs are born into the darkness of hibernation.

Nature does not hurry, yet everything is accomplished.

— Lao Tzu

MEDICINE JOURNEY
Rest Retrieval

Find a comfortable place to sit or lie down and begin to breathe. Set the intention to retrieve the aspects of yourself that know the power of rest. Call on Bear to assist you on this journey. A Great Mother Bear appears before you; you feel or sense their presence as they stand there, strong and powerful. They ask you to take a moment to feel into your capacity. Assess your heart, your mind, your body, your Spirit. How full or empty are you? Are you filled to the brim? Or do you have spaciousness? Take a full and deep breath to acknowledge this awareness.

Mother Bear leads you into a den that has been created for you. It is filled with the most comforting things you can imagine and, as you enter, you feel your nervous system relaxing and your breath gradually softening. There is a cozy healing bed that has been created for you, and you lie down. A Medicine Guide and Healer walks over to you and places their hands on the top of your head, cradling it, and you feel a surge of warmth as you are held in their hands. You feel yourself unclenching, unraveling, and releasing. Is there anything that is no longer in alignment with your path? Begin to unwind it out of your system. Where can you let go? Let it be seen and acknowledged in this space so that you can start to release. Feel your system beginning to shed and release what is no longer needed and release it into the Earth. Sink into rest.

Mother Bear walks over to you and, in their claw, they hold bear grease: a profoundly healing salve. They offer this to you, and it begins to lubricate your organs, tissues, and bones. It sinks in deeply, especially nourishing your adrenals and moving into every vertebra of your spine. She wraps an energetic fur around your body, which feels so warm and comforting. You lay in this bed with this healing Medicine of rest informing you. *You are the Medicine.* When you feel ready, you stand up, start your journey back out of this den, and slowly come back into your body.

If you can lie down for a few moments after this journey, take a nap, or go to bed, this might be a beautiful time to do so. Let Bear Medicine continue to move through you as you integrate this Medicine. Surprisingly, even laying down flat on your back for a couple of minutes will inform your body that it is safe to stop and rest. I practice this a few times per day to create new neural pathways to give my body permission to rest.

Medicine Reflection: What was unwound from your system? Check in with your capacity. How does it feel now?

Honoring the Void

During the COVID-19 pandemic I was trying to homeschool my kids, run my business, parent, and everything else that comes with adulting. There were times when I felt grief and sadness about the impact of that time on my family and my children. It has taken a toll on everyone, of course, and I am mindful that this is a collective experience with some people struggling with much more grief than what I am feeling.

But one weekend nearly a year after the first lockdown, I felt an old and familiar darkness rising within me. Even before the pandemic, this would happen every year in the late Winter and a friend would tell me it was my "dark night of the soul." A phrase that has been used to describe disorientation around one's identity or a spiritual crisis, the "dark night of the soul" is a state that was initially described in a poem by 16th-century Spanish mystic and poet, St. John of the Cross.

For many years I would find myself cuddled under a blanket, feeling sad and with lower energy than usual during these times. I would shame myself, wondering what was wrong with me. Why didn't I feel the same inspiration I felt in the Spring or Summer? Why couldn't I just push through and "get over it"? I would doubt my life path as a Healer and homeopath and tell my husband that I was giving it all up to go work at my local bookstore. The people at the bookstore looked so calm and happy. When I started feeling the same thing that weekend during COVID, I was able to see it for what it was: this darkness was coming to be experienced and validated as a necessary season or cycle. The more I resisted it, shamed myself, or tried to push through, the longer it would last. So, this time, instead, I sent gratitude to my body for its fatigue. I honored my need to cry, and I welcomed in more cozy snuggles and movies with my children. This time feels like a dark void to me, and with the additional stress of the pandemic, it felt a bit like a time warp. I have gone through this same experience enough to know that if I honor this season with love, I will come out on the other side with beautiful new seeds to plant and ideas to co-create. While I am still learning to love the void, at least now I can trust that this season doesn't last forever.

YOUR ANCESTRAL PULSE

We come by our disrupted relationship to rest honestly. Often, our patterns and wounds around resting are inherited and passed down generationally. Combine that with the current capitalistic and patriarchal power structure that tells us to keep on producing, and it's a recipe for burnout. Ancestrally, BIPOC (Black, Indigenous, People of Color) have deep intergenerational trauma around rest, woven into their cells. In the folks I work with, this trauma often is rooted in the colonizer and oppressor forcing labor, enslavement, and servitude. The impact of this dynamic is still felt in our system today as capitalism and white supremacy keep these wounds alive with daily triggers and reminders. In my own journey of unraveling the impacts of colonization, I often feel the effect that residential schools had on my lineage and how that continues to show up as the part of me that pushes, hustles, and drives herself to burnout. I have energetically traveled back to times before first settler contact in my exploration of healing through these wounds. In those journeys, I have found beautiful healing and reclaimed our original ways around rest. We listened to the seasons and cycles; we took rest when needed; and we knew the power of our nighttime dreams, and what came from quiet moments of daydreaming. I've filled myself up with the original instructions of how my Ancestors related to rest and allowed the pulse of this to inform my healing. It's a daily journey of reclamation and one that I am deeply committed to. I wish to break the cycles of burnout for the next generation.

Some ways that you may have internalized capitalism include:

- Prioritizing productivity over rest.
- Feeling guilty for taking a vacation or a break.

- Basing your worth on whether you succeed at something (your career, your social media metrics, your accomplishments).

- Pushing past your capacity and not listening to your body.

- Shaming yourself for not being productive, even if you are moving through struggle.

> **Medicine Reflection:** Is there any trauma in your lineage that you know of that could impact your relationship to rest? How might you shift or heal that narrative in your system?

THE GREAT MYSTERY

As Indigenous people, we speak of the Great Mystery that surrounds us, moves through us, and holds us. In my understanding, this is a consciousness that carries the potential for healing and miracles to weave through our lives. This consciousness moves "behind the scenes," so to speak, and we can tune in to it more effectively in times of quiet or rest. I have experienced it as an energetic pulse that is birthed from the void. In my vision, it is spacious and appears as galaxies upon galaxies. Over my lifetime, I have come to trust that there is potency in the unseen. When we can truly let go and surrender to rest, the Great Mystery can meet us. Bear Medicine carries this magic, reminding us of these unseen forces that are at play when we take the time we need. Miraculous things happen daily. Sometimes we need to stop and listen to let them in.

When I was in private practice as a homeopath, certain weeks would get slow. Bookings would decrease, or people would cancel, and I would freak out. *My business is failing*, I would think. I would sink into despair and feel like, somehow, life was falling apart. Over the years, I began to trust in the power of the Great Mystery that would co-create these times with me. This space was necessary for my next stage of growth.

Don't leap out, my soul would whisper. *Not yet.* This liminal, disorienting space was Medicine for me, a space of my becoming. It was a rite of passage, and when I resisted it, it would become painful. When I surrendered to it, it became beautiful. The Great Mystery is always working behind the scenes with us and for us. Our job is to trust the process and call in the light of Bear Moon to nourish us.

Bear Medicine Invocation

Dearest Bear, I invite you to help me fine-tune my body's awareness when I need rest. Remind me that it's safe for me to do so. May I remember that miracles come from sinking into the void. I am grateful for the Bear grease you offered to lubricate my essence. When I need reminders, please surround me with your warm fur, helping me to feel worthy of taking the time I need for myself. I commit to listening to my natural seasons and cycles and trust in my body's knowing and the Great Mystery.

Mkwa Giizis Moon Affirmation

As I let go and sink into rest, the Great Mystery moves through me. I break cycles of burnout and welcome in healing. In my restoration, I am enough. I am the Medicine.

○)))) ● ● (((((◯ ◯

CHAPTER 4

ZIISBAAKDOKE GIIZIS SUGAR MOON

Our third Moon of Creation is in March, when the snow begins to melt and the sweet Maple Tree sap begins to run. Maple syrup is a traditional Medicine for Indigenous people offered to us to balance our blood. We honor this Medicine as a deep healing tonic. This Moon asks us to reflect on the sweetness in our lives that flows to us through the words we speak to ourselves and the beliefs we hold about our worth. Unconditional love is an antidote to our inner critic, and this Moon reminds us that compassion heals all. During this Moon, we celebrate the Spring Equinox, Creation begins to unfreeze and melt, and new life is born.

MOON LEGEND: HOW THE MAPLE TREE FOUND ITS MEDICINE

In the beginning, the Trees started as tiny seeds. In their seed state, they began to dream of what they could be one day. Pine shared that they wanted to offer a beautiful fragrance to the forest so that all who walked there would remember them. Birch spoke about traveling on the Water and dreamed of being transformed into material for a canoe. Oak was a hopeful being, believing that anything was possible, and they wanted to share that with all who found their acorns. When it came time for Maple to share, they found that they didn't have a vision of their future.

The other Trees taunted Maple. "Without a dream for who you are becoming, you are worthless and insignificant." Maple felt their heart sink; they felt lost and directionless. They wondered what was wrong with them. Why were they devoid of dream and vision? Were they even good enough to be a Tree? They felt like a fraud.

Of course, the cycles of nature continued, as they do, and Maple was watered by the rain and fed by the Sun. As they grew into a sapling and then a young tree, the birds watched Maple with curiosity. They could see the beauty that Maple carried and the potential they held. Every day they would come and try to uplift Maple. They surrounded the Tree with love, friendship, and support. The birds tried to come up with some ideas for the vision of Maple's becoming:

"Maybe you could bear fruit for the Animals," said Cardinal. "Or perhaps you could provide shade for all our Kin," offered Blue Jay. Maple wasn't convinced. They had taken the criticism of their fellow Trees deeply into their heart, and they simply couldn't see beyond that. They thanked their bird friends for trying so hard to uplift them, but alas, their inner critic took over, and they felt stuck as an imposter.

The birds would continue to visit Maple daily, offering encouragement and support. One day, it was stormy, and a great wind swept into the Forest. It was so strong it carried the birds in its vortex, swirling them all around, lifting them, and then dropping them to the ground. Maple gasped as all of their beautiful bird friends fell to the Earth unconscious. Immediately, they scooped all the birds up with their loving branches and comforting leaves. Wrapping deep compassion around the birds, Maple began to weep. Maple cried tears of pain that had been stuck in their heart since they were a seedling. They shook with grief about all of the times the birds tried to tell them how beautiful they were, and they didn't listen. Maple cried and cried and cried, their tears washing over the bodies of the birds.

Just when they thought they couldn't cry any longer, something magical started to happen, the birds, soaked with the tears of the Maple Tree, started to come back to life. They opened their eyes and began to sing the most beautiful songs. "You healed us with your tears, dear Maple!" they cried. "The Water that flows through your veins is magical! It's sweet and nourishing nectar that can heal bodies and hearts. You are a Healer!"

Maple couldn't believe it! The vision and dream of who they were meant to be finally manifested. Through the release of their pain and grief, they could finally see their gifts and worth. The fellow Trees, witnessing what had happened, gathered around Maple in awe. "We are deeply sorry that we harmed you with our words, dear sibling, we see you, we honor you." From that day forward, the sap that flowed through Maple's body would be Medicine for all that tasted it, and the Maple Tree stood in complete confidence, seeing that it was sweetness, not harshness, that would heal.

Animal Spirit: *Waawaashkeshi* (Deer)

The Animal Spirit that best represents the third Moon is the Deer, or as they are known in Anishiinabemowin,

Waawaashkeshi. Maple provides sap filled with sweetness and nourishment, which mirrors the Medicine that Deer brings to our hearts. Deer stands with quiet grace and humble power, an energy our world needs more of. I believe that we enter this world connected to the source of unconditional love. If we don't get our needs met as children, this connection starts to break down gradually. We hear harsh words, and they become our inner voice. We base our worthiness on how much we give or do, and love becomes conditional. Deer is here to remind us to soften into grace, love ourselves as we are, and honor our worthiness. We all deserve kind and loving treatment in our lives, and Deer helps us release the parts that shame so that we can meet ourselves with more gentleness and compassion. Just like the Medicine of maple syrup, Deer brings in sweetness.

Deer Message

- You are perfect in your imperfections.
- You are loveable, unconditionally.
- Meet your mistakes with grace.
- You are enough.

THE INNER CRITIC

In clients who I have mentored, the feeling of not being "enough"—a lack of self-confidence, low self-worth, and feelings of imperfection—is what holds them back from taking steps toward their dreams. They share that they desire to speak on stages, leave their jobs to start a business, be more visible, share their gifts, or engage in meaningful relationships. Their insecurities range from not feeling educated enough, healthy enough, or beautiful enough, to feeling like a fraud and wondering, "Who am I to share my gifts with the world?" In my experience, these feelings stem from shame and trauma and are often tied to childhood wounding and societal expectations.

My inner critic is something that I have repeatedly met with deep compassion. Living with an autoimmune condition, I have realized that holding this compassion for myself is a big part of my healing. In treating others with autoimmune diseases, I have found this same pattern to be true.

Here are some ways the inner critic may show up in our lives:

- feeling like what we do is never enough.

- beating ourselves up for perceived mistakes or imperfections.

- speaking harsh words about aspects of ourselves.

- punishing ourselves when something goes "wrong."

A question that I've found helpful to ask myself or others when the inner critic is at the forefront is this:

Whose voice is this?

Our parents' voices and words become beliefs in our hearts. Societal and collective messages become ingrained in our minds. Experiences with teachers, friends, relatives, acquaintances, and our whole outer world can shape our inner world. So much so that when we find ourselves shaming, blaming, or criticizing ourselves, the harsh voice at the helm may be as a result of something that deeply hurt us in the past. As a child, we didn't have the tools that we now do as an adult to process through pain. What can appear to be a seemingly small hurt through the eyes of an adult can be soul-crushing for a child.

As a child, I was highly sensitive to the tone of voice people used. If someone raised their voice to me, I immediately thought I was in trouble. I remember being seven years old, in Grade 2, and we had a substitute teacher for the day. He had instructed us that we must put our hand up to get out of our seats. It was snack time, and I had just finished my apple. I got up, as I always do, to throw the core in the garbage. I remember him yelling at me to sit back down and mocking me that I didn't listen properly. My cheeks burned with embarrassment, and tears entered my eyes. From that moment on, I was conscientious to always to follow the rules and never push back. His words and tone of voice became part of my inner world. Whenever I would "mess up," I would speak to myself in that same harsh, taunting voice.

I was only seven. I didn't have the years of healing and training and experience that I do now to meet myself with the compassion I deserved. A part of that teacher's insensitive voice and callous way froze inside of me back then, and it's taken many years of thawing and chipping away at that moment to break that seven-year-old self free from the ice and lift her up into healing. I share this because I believe we all have these "little" events that happen in our lives that we are not fully capable of healing through at that moment. Gradually these events start to grow and begin to tear down our sense of self. The time of Sugar Moon reminds us that we are worthy of being treated with care. It can feel like a long journey back to gentleness when our inner critic speaks with the voice of our most painful memories, but with time, acknowledgment, and clarity, we can eventually lean into the softness and self-love that we so deserve.

UNCONDITIONAL LOVE

We are born of the divine. Pure essence, beaming with love. We come into this world inherently worthy and then, somewhere along the way, this knowing begins to unravel. As we grow, we may start to perceive that our worth is conditional. If our parents have unmet needs of their own, their wounding gets projected onto our path. When love is not readily available, we will do anything in order to receive what we need. For a child, it's survival.

As we grow, we learn how to compensate, maybe we close our heart in protection, or perhaps we try to please everyone around us so that nobody will abandon us. Maybe we become perfectionists or shrink away from our biggest dreams because we don't want to fail. Love becomes conditional, based on what we do, how we act, and what we give. We forget our inherent worth and that our very existence is more than enough. We strive to become "better" or "perfect" and put our lives on hold until we deem ourselves acceptable. So, how do we begin to love ourselves unconditionally when the world models something very different for us? How do we come back to remembering that we don't need to do anything to prove ourselves loveable?

Four Ways to Love Yourself Unconditionally

1. *Unweave yourself from the story of conditional worth.*

   Both white supremacy and patriarchal conditioning have falsely told us that we are only worthy when producing, accomplishing new heights, or gaining status somehow. Dr. Valerie Rein coined the term PSD and wrote the book *Patriarchy Stress Disorder* to describe the Ancestral and collective trauma that affects those who identify as women. She believes that this prevents us from stepping into our joyful success and fulfillment.

As a student of her work, I can say that unweaving the energies a person has been marinating in for an entire lifetime is deep work. Furthermore, as a BIPOC person doing this work, I have found that unraveling the massive generational trauma takes time. We all marinate in white supremacy, born into this society, but BIPOC folks carry a depth of trauma that vibrates in our bones and blood memory. Dr. Valerie and her partner, Jeffrey Tambor, shared a unique blend of nervous system and energetic practices, which I have found helpful as I reclaim my right to take up space and feel healthy entitlement simply because I exist. We all deserve to unweave from the lie that we are only worthy when we work ourselves beyond our capacity or achieve things that society deems successful.

Medicine Reflection: Have you bought into the lie that your worth is dependent on how productive or outwardly "successful" you are? What trauma might you carry in your lineage that continues to feed this myth?

2. *Look at the systems that surround you.*

How often have you heard the term "imposter syndrome"? How many times have you felt that you carry this? It's a diagnosis given to women that describes the feeling you have when you feel like a fraud or are filled with self-doubt. An article published by the *Harvard Business Review,* titled "Stop Telling Women They Have Imposter Syndrome," shared that this "diagnosis" can be harmful, as it blames the individual versus looking at the systemic issues at play. Therefore, so-called imposter syndrome implies that the woman is the issue instead of the historical and cultural contexts surrounding women.

Systemic racism amplifies these issues for women of color, setting us up to feel like we don't measure up to patriarchal, Eurocentric standards. So, perhaps you don't suffer from imposter syndrome, but rather the environment in which you try to function does not have the vision of diversity, equity, and inclusion that includes you. It's not your fault. Systems need to change.

Medicine Reflection: Have you ever felt like a "fraud" or shamed yourself for feeling self-doubt? Was the environment supportive and set up for you to succeed?

3. *Locate your inner oppressor.*

For many years I would meditate, and see images of nuns, priests, and missionaries. Their energy was stern and oppressive, and it would take my breath away. When I started to heal through some of the generational trauma of the impact of residential schools and colonization, I began to see that the images were deeply embedded in my cellular memory, inherited through my DNA. Sadly, the voice of the oppressor was often tangled with my own voice. When I finally discerned the difference, I could begin to heal what was mine and what was inherited.

I learned about the term "inner oppressor" from Leesa Renee Hall, a writer and mental health advocate. When I heard this term, everything about my inner critic seemed to make sense. The oppressive, colonized, and racist treatment Indigenous people have endured (and continue to endure) have embedded so deeply into my psyche that I have not always treated myself with unconditional love. Seeing this truth helped me understand that it was not my fault that I was so harsh with myself—but now it was my responsibility to heal these layers so that my children and descendants don't have to.

Medicine Reflection: Do you have an "inner oppressor"? What do they say to you?

4. *Hold your shame with compassion.*

In the years that I held space listening to my patients' stories, the one emotion that seemed to be the hardest to access was shame. People could identify grief, anger, joy, or fear, but shame seemed like a challenge for most. Shame researcher and author Brené Brown defines shame as a deeply painful sensation, experience, or belief that we are flawed because of something we have done. She says that this leads us to feel like we are unworthy of connection and love. When we marinate in shame, we believe that we are unworthy of belonging. Belonging is a biological need, and therefore, shame separates us from feeling safe in this world.

One of the practices that I have developed over the years is to meet the shame that arises with compassion. Like many of my clients, I had a hard time naming the feeling I was experiencing as shame. But once I did, I noticed that even though it was a profoundly uncomfortable sensation, if I acknowledged it, validated it, and then met it with compassion, it would move through me. Deer Medicine has always helped me with this, softening all that is harsh within.

Another practice I walk with is to share with my "shame siblings." I have a few close people in my life with whom I can share what I feel to be my biggest mistakes, flaws, and insecurities. Speaking these vulnerable thoughts out loud to someone who holds my heart with tenderness is so healing for me. I realize that it is a great privilege to be able to have these relationships in my life. If you find that you don't have this in your inner circle, journaling is a great way to start a practice of holding your shame outside of your body.

> **Medicine Reflection:** Is there an experience that you can recall where you felt shame? How did it feel in your body?

ACCIDENTS HAPPEN

When I was a child and would spill milk or make a mistake, my mother would say these two beautiful words: "Accidents happen." It's true. They do. We all make mistakes, and we all learn from those mistakes. I recently read and filled out the *Big Life Journal for Kids* with my son, and two colorful pages stood out to me. One said: "Mistakes are proof that you are trying." And the other said: "Did you know mistakes grow your brain?" It went on to say that when you do something "right" your brain doesn't grow. A part of me knew this, but a more significant part of me needed this reminder. Mistakes help us grow. If we did everything well all the time, we would stagnate.

A few years ago, I played in a piano recital and, as I sat there awkwardly on stage, I forgot my entire piece. I messed up huge! Even as an adult playing in a recital, I felt ashamed and embarrassed. I ran out of there as quickly as I could. I had practiced this piece for a year and played it well at home, of course. I told a friend, and she said, "Asha, perfect people are annoying!" I laughed at how seriously I was taking myself. Accidents happen, and mistakes help you grow—two lessons I will continue to integrate into my life, with Deer Medicine at my side.

BODY SHAME

The first symptom that showed up after I was diagnosed with lupus was strange skin rashes. The doctors said they were part of the illness and that I would have to just deal with them. As a teenager, I found this so challenging. I would have these breakouts that would cause redness and scarring. I felt deeply ashamed of my skin and, most days, didn't want to look in the mirror. Over the years, lupus has caused hair loss, joint deformities in my hands and feet, and other manifestations that have caused me to feel different from what the world deems beautiful. I remember in my 20s feeling ashamed when someone asked if I was tired because of how I looked. The shame I've carried in my body from having a chronic illness has opened up a daily journey toward loving myself in all of my perceived imperfections.

I know that my story is relatable for so many, as media and current culture norms condition us to meet certain perfection standards when it comes to our bodies. This shame is based on our perception of what a desirable body should look or feel like. For me, the shame comes from not being what society deems as perfectly "healthy." In her book *The Body Is Not an Apology*, Sonya Renee Taylor says society's insistence that all bodies should be healthy is damaging. "Health is not a state we owe the world. We are not less valuable, worthy, or loveable because we are not healthy. Lastly, no standard of health is achievable for all bodies." When I read this, I took a deep breath. There are so many ways that our bodies have been shamed and so many ways that we have soaked up these messages. Relating to our bodies as a friend and ally can go a long way in our healing.

And I said to my body. Softly. 'I want to be your friend.'
It took a long breath. And replied. 'I have
been waiting my whole life for this.'

— NAYYIRAH WAHEED

MEDICINE JOURNEY
Body Compassion with Deer

Years ago, I was in Shamanic Training with an Algonquin Medicine Healer and participated in a version of this healing practice that I now integrate into my days. I will never forget the first time I practiced this. I sobbed as I remembered how worthy my body was of hearing these words. May my version serve your beautiful reconnection with your body.

1. Bring your hands together and close your eyes for a moment. Envision light blasting out of your hands. This light is the same force that heals you when you cut yourself, a vital force of Medicine.

2. Ask Deer Spirit to be your ally for this self-love healing. Deer surrounds you in a protective bubble of love.

3. Place your hands on your belly. Begin to send compassion and forgiveness messages to your body. Here are some examples of what you might say:

    I'm so sorry for all the times I have put you down.
    I'm so sorry for all the times I have not listened to your calls for help.
    I'm so sorry for shaming you, blaming you, criticizing you.
    I'm so sorry for the times I have not loved you.
    (Add anything else that feels relevant to your own story with your body.)

4. Feel the compassion of your words and the light from your hands pouring out into your body. Move your hands around your body where you feel guided. Start infusing the phrase *I am sorry,*

I love you, I am sorry, I love you, I am sorry, I love you as you move your hands around.

5. Envision all the harsh and critical energy within softening, making space and room for more love and less shame.

A gentle reminder that none of this is your "fault." The systems currently in place are working to keep you stuck in shame and disconnected from your true divinity. You are loveable. You are beautiful as you are.

THE MEDICINE OF MAPLE SYRUP

For Indigenous people, Maple syrup is honored for its sweet taste and medicinal properties. It has been harvested for thousands of years and is one of the first Medicines harvested each year. When the Europeans settled on the Lands that I call home, Maples were often cleared from the Land, which strained our relationship to this Medicine. Like many of our Ceremonies and practices, colonization impacted our sacred connection—reclaiming something as simple as my relationship to maple syrup and teaching my children about its value helps to mend the damage done. The Sugar Moon brings us back to this connection of sweetness.

In the early Spring, my *Mishomis* (Grandfather) would go into the sugar bush of our home territory to help gather sap from the Maple trees. I remember going with him one year and marveling at how much sap you need to collect to make maple syrup. When I receive Maple syrup from my home territory of *Neyaashiinigmiing*, I am deeply grateful, knowing that it was from the Trees and Land where my Spirit lives. Each drop of sweetness is reclamation Medicine for my heart and Spirit. When I consume this as Medicine, I welcome it into my body as an Ancestral gift. I am reminded that I am enough, that my Ancestors dreamed me here. The Sugar Moon connects us to the time of this gathering when the sap begins to run, and we are reconnected to the nourishment available to us. It's a sacred time. Maple syrup reminds me to be kind to my body and that every part is loveable. It moves me from shame to love.

SWEETNESS AS MEDICINE

A few years ago, I read some work by psychologist and author Dr. Mario Martinez, who spoke about his theories around why the Tibetan lamas he was working with had a high incidence of diabetes. I was curious about his thoughts, as Indigenous people of Turtle Island also have an increased incidence of diabetes. Martinez feels that this issue is partly a result of bypassing anger and jumping into instant forgiveness. The effect of not fully feeling or expressing anger releases endorphins that eventually highjack the body's ability to process glucose in effective ways.

When I read this, I thought about the anger that Indigenous people rightly deserve to feel. The impact of attempted genocide, the lack of clean Water on First Nations, the horrific generational implications of residential schools, and so much more. I have wondered where all that anger has gone. Could we ever fully process it? Could we ever fully express it? Could we ever truly heal through this as we see our youth dying from suicide and alcohol destroying families? Do we have the emotional capacity to truly and deeply feel this?

I wonder about what is needed to heal these generational wounds. I wonder what the antidote to the pain could be. As Indigenous people, we have always needed more sweetness. Is the rampant state of diabetes in our communities a cry for this unmet need? Could acknowledgment, validation, and compassion for suffering be the Medicine that we, as a people, need to heal through these generational wounds? I wish I knew.

What I do know is that trying to eradicate cultural traditions, language, and spiritual beliefs while also taking love away from children has lasting impacts. I imagine what could have been if children were met with kindness and compassion instead of violence. I imagine what could be if our people who are suffering from addiction were met with loving arms instead of incarceration. I imagine what could be if our youth were told every day that we see them and they are important. This is sweetness and I believe it is the deep Medicine that we need to heal the atrocities of the past. Perhaps when we meet each other's pain in this way, we can heal together.

Medicine Reflection: What parts of you are calling for sweetness?

Deer Medicine Invocation

Dearest Deer, I invite you to soften the inner critic that rises within. Help me to see that I am infinitely worthy of divine love and care. Remind me of my perfection when all I see are imperfections. Surround me with unconditional love. Help me to offer my physical body gentleness and kindness when shame arises. Root me back into my worth when I feel doubt. I am grateful for your beauty, grace, and love.

Ziisbaakdoke Giizis Moon Affirmation

I am loveable and worthy as I am. Gentleness and unconditional love heal me. Enough in every way, I am the Medicine.

CHAPTER 5

NAMEBINE GIIZIS SUCKERFISH MOON

Our fourth Moon of Creation represents our teachings of purification and cleansing, including Smoke Medicine. It is a time to reflect on how we can remain clear vessels of our highest expression in mind, body, and Spirit. This Moon occurs in April at a time when there is more daylight in the Northern Hemisphere, the snow is melting, and the buds are starting to appear. It's a time of freshness and new beginnings, so we must approach this time by clearing away what is no longer needed.

MOON LEGEND: HOW SUCKERFISH BROUGHT TEACHINGS TO THE PEOPLE

When the Earth was beginning to awaken, and slight hints of color were sprouting up all around, Suckerfish swam happily in the Waters. Suckerfish had an incredible ability to reproduce—a beautiful gift offered to them by Creator. A generous fish, Suckerfish gave up their lives so that the Anishinaabe people wouldn't starve.

As Suckerfish swam and fed the Anishinaabe people, they began to feel a new purpose coming forward—they noticed that the people were becoming more and more disconnected from their true nature and the Spirit World. Suckerfish had a beautiful relationship with Creator and knew their place as a Water Spirit and helper. They prayed to Creator to ask how they could serve in the highest way. In response, Creator placed a pathway of Stars down to the Water, and Suckerfish traveled a long way to the Spirit World. There Suckerfish learned about the Plant Medicines that could help the people cleanse, purify, and come back home to their hearts and renew their connection with the Spirit World.

When they were ready to share the teachings, Suckerfish made the long journey back down to the Earth and brought the wisdom that the people needed. Every time the Ojibwe people would interact with Suckerfish, they would receive the purification and cleansing teachings that continue to be used to this day. The people made a promise that they would hold the wisdom in sacred ways to honor the long journey Suckerfish made to retrieve them fully.

Animal Spirit: *Omagakii* (Frog)

The Animal Spirit that best represents our Fourth Moon is Frog or, as they are known in Anishiinabemowin, *Omagakii*. While Suckerfish brought this knowledge to the people, it's Frog who embodies those teachings with its vital Medicine of cleansing and purification.

Frog moves with us through this Moon phase to teach us that in order to maintain balance within our physical, emotional, and spiritual bodies, we need to cleanse ourselves consistently and intentionally. Frog is intimately connected to the element of Water, an essential and sacred part of

Creation for Indigenous people. Water carries its own Spirit and has infinite power to cleanse. Therefore, Frog reflects to us what needs to be purified and cleared out so that we can remain in balance.

Frog Message

- Assess the clutter in your life in your home spaces, inner thoughts, and physical body.

- Honor your emotions, especially your sacred Water, which is expressed through tears.

- Embrace transformation and metamorphosis, from stagnation to rebirth.

- Prioritize purifying or detoxifying your energy, heart, and mind.

HONORING SMOKE MEDICINE

One of the ways that Indigenous people listen to the call of Frog and purify and cleanse is with the use of our Sacred Medicines: Tobacco, Cedar, Sweetgrass, and Sage. Some of the most beautiful memories of my life involve the lighting of these sacred Medicines. My Indigenous heart and Spirit feel instantly connected when the smoke begins to fill our space. I can feel our Spirit helpers and Ancestors gathering, and many times, tears run down my face. Lighting Medicines for our smudge Ceremonies are more than just "cleansing"; the ritual is a remembering of all we have lost, and of all we have reclaimed.

There are two memories of this Ceremony that will stir up emotion in me even though years have passed. The first was during my naming Ceremony. I will never forget the sound of the match striking up the Medicine. I will never forget the Anishinaabe words *Mishomis* (my Grandfather) spoke, in our original language, as he called to our Ancestors to receive my Spirit name. I will always remember my tears and the scent of the Medicines weaving through my nose and lungs.

My other memory was of my wedding day. My Mother held my new Eagle Feather, a gift from my Father. As she moved the smoke around my new Jewish family, I could feel our two groups of Ancestors coming together, gathering and coming forward in pain and love, trauma and healing. The smoke initiated a new healing vision for all of us that day. We would break cycles together. We would dream of a new way. I felt my aunt, who had recently passed, join us from the Spirit World, and knew that she was blessing our union. Smudge does that. It offers prayer, possibility, miracles, and remembering. And for me, tears. Always tears.

Indigenous people worldwide have known about the power of burning medicinal plants as a sacred way to cleanse. In many places in North America, this practice is called smudging, and different Nations practice this in their way. It is a Ceremony that is passed down from one generation to the next. It is important to note that not all Indigenous people practice smudging, as some Nations did not adopt this Ceremony into their Medicine ways. The tradition that I have learned and will be sharing is through my Anishinaabe Elders, teachers, and blood memory. The word "smudge" is traditionally used by Indigenous people and is a culturally specific practice. Therefore, I prefer to use the term "Smoke Medicine" when teaching non-Indigenous folks how to cleanse. If this doesn't resonate with you, perhaps find a term used by your Ancestors that aligns better.

A way to properly honor and respect our traditions is to know the history behind them. In Canada, from 1884 to

1951, Ceremonies such as the Potlach Ceremony and the Sundance Ceremony were outlawed. The government believed that the way toward assimilation was to prohibit and therefore extinguish certain Ceremonies. So even though smudging itself wasn't explicitly banned, our connection to it was questioned when we observed other Ceremonies being taken away from our brother and sister Nations. Our people are resilient, and many practices have since been reclaimed, but it continues to be a journey to move through the trauma of colonization and mend all that was broken.

This is why it can be painful for many Indigenous people to see our Medicines turned into a trend. So much has been taken. So much pain inflicted. Over the years, I have facilitated healing for many non-Indigenous folks. The most beautiful thing that I have observed is the proper reverence and honoring these people hold for our Ceremonies once they know the truth of our history. I am grateful to be a bridge and Wisdom Keeper to invite folks who are not Indigenous to become allies. I have always said that it is not up to me to judge what people choose to do. I believe that it is between you and Creator.

ON CEREMONY

In my lifetime, I have learned that Ceremony starts from within. We walk in Ceremony every day. Every intention, step, word, and breath can become a Ceremony, and I intend that these offerings bring more presence, peace, connection, and honoring to your life. If you are a ceremonialist and create grand altars and brilliant sacred spaces for your rituals, I honor this. However, those are not necessities if they're not accessible for you. We can approach a Ceremony with simplicity.

Some of the most vital Ceremonies of my life have happened in places you would least expect. A Ceremony is something that helps you connect more deeply with your sacred self. Yes, I've done Ceremony in the mountains of Peru or sat with the Fire with my Elders, but I've also experienced Ceremony while sobbing on my bedroom floor. Whether I was in a cave in New Mexico, a basement in Lake Titicaca, or at home, looking into my children's eyes for the first time, it's all been ceremonial. An Elder once told me that it was like an energetic sweat lodge every time I've gone through immense physical pain. I have gone through vision quests in my own heart and cracked open the deepest parts of my Spirit and wisdom through daily life experience. I believe that these experiences are available to all of us, and although I share specific guidance and protocols in this chapter, I believe that we don't always need fancy tools or altars to make it meaningful.

Perhaps prayer is just poetry, and we are living the expressions of what it means to be human. This is why Creator gave us gifts to remember. This is why, when I burn sage or lay Tobacco down, I know that I am tethered to a love that has remained steady throughout the centuries and that always calls me back to its own sacredness. And that sacredness will always lead me back out to the world to do the work of love. Prayer is always an invitation.

— KAITLIN B. CURTICE, *Native: Identity, Belonging, and Rediscovering God*

THE ELEMENTAL POWER OF SMOKE CEREMONY

Smoke Medicine can be used for many different reasons. We use it to purify our minds so that we may think positive thoughts about ourselves and others. When we are speaking critically to ourselves, lighting some Smoke Medicine can bring about a shift and awareness to be more loving and compassionate. There are times in our lives when we may find that we're angry, and while there may be a good reason for our anger, we can use Smoke Medicine to help neutralize the intensity so that we can find balance, ease, and perhaps even forgiveness more quickly.

We can use Smoke Medicine to cleanse ourselves of energy that we have taken on for others. Frog Medicine reminds us to do this often. I find this absorption of energy happens a lot for those who identify as empathic, highly sensitive, or open-hearted souls who want to help. A sacred smoke Ceremony will allow those energies that are not yours to carry to be cleared from your energy field. I light Medicine every morning and smudge my family before they start their day to help keep them protected and safe. When I had my private practice in my home, sacred smudge was burning all day to ensure I kept my energy and that of my space clear and pure. The light of Suckerfish Moon calls us to be diligent with our energy hygiene so that we walk in clarity and connection. The most beautiful way that Smoke Medicine is used in my life and the lives of many Indigenous people is that it instantly opens our connection to the Spirit World. The scent of the burning plants immediately connects us to the knowing and wisdom that we are related to every being upon this Earth. In that remembering, we treat each Animal, Plant, Stone, Waterdrop, and Human Being with reverence. Sacred smoke reminds us of our spiritual connection and how we are much more than our physical experience.

Traditionally, this Ceremony incorporates the four elements, Earth, Air, Water, and Fire.

- ***Earth (represented by Sage, Sweetgrass, Cedar, and Tobacco)***

  We source these Medicines from Mother Earth with gratitude and respect, honoring that she is gifting them to us. As Indigenous people, we don't believe that we own the Earth. We work to be reciprocal in our interactions, always. I like to see the Plants we use in our Ceremony as sacred beings with their own Spirits.

- ***Air (represented by a feather)***

  Traditionally, we use an Eagle feather in our smudge Ceremonies as the Eagle is the bird that takes our prayers up to Creator. The fanning of the feather creates quickening energy, much like the essence of wind. I like to envision that the wind created by the feather activates and amplifies the prayers or intentions that we are setting.

- ***Water (represented by an abalone shell)***

  Abalone shells can withstand the high heat. Without Water, we would not have life, and the shell represents this Creation energy. I like to think of it as a womb, holding the essence of what we are birthing or intending.

- ***Fire (represented by smoke and flame)***

  Fire Medicine holds the power of transmutation and regeneration. I like to think of the fire element in this Ceremony as holding the energy of possibility. When we burn away the old, a new way opens up.

THE FOUR SACRED MEDICINES

Traditionally, there are four Plant Medicines that we have used for our smudge Ceremony. As I speak of my connection to this Ceremony as an Indigenous person, I will be using the word "smudge" throughout this section. As I mentioned earlier in this chapter, I have offered the words "Smoke Medicine" as a respectful alternative for non-Indigenous readers. The Medicines are Tobacco, Cedar, Sweetgrass, and Sage, and they have many uses other than our smudge Ceremony. The use of these Medicines brings a deep spiritual connection, awakening, and remembering as soon as they are picked up, burned, or used for healing.

Asemaa (Tobacco)

One beautiful Spring day, the ice had melted, and the Waters were beginning to run. My Mother and I went out for a walk, and she tucked some Medicine into her pocket. When we got to the river, she handed me some, and she shared the power of placing Tobacco in running Water. She shared that the Water spirits take our prayers to the Animals, the Rocks, the riverbeds. They are here to witness our gratitude and intentions. I always remember that teaching and bring Tobacco anytime I go to the Water so that my prayers may spread to all of my Relations.

Tobacco is said to be the first gift we received from Creator. Indigenous people have held this Plant as sacred, and we use it as an offering to a Medicine Person/Elder/Healer for guidance. We use it as offerings to the Earth in gratitude and smoke it in our Pipe Ceremonies. Every morning, I will go outside with my sons and make a Tobacco offering. I ask them what they are grateful for, and they place their prayers down into the Earth. Sadly, most people hear "Tobacco" and think of smoking cigarettes. Most of us are aware of the harmful chemicals in commercial cigarettes, but for the purpose of this discussion, it is important to note that this was never the original intent of this Medicine, and this would have been considered disrespectful of the use of the Plant. Instead in our smudge, it represents gratitude and an offering to the Spirit World. Whenever I share this teaching in schools, I always love seeing the curiosity in children's faces, upon hearing Tobacco described in a new way. I hold a vision that they will create a respectful relationship with it and view it in its authentic, original healing form.

Giizhik (Cedar)

When I did my vision quest, the Medicine Man told me a story: "One time, I was doing a vision quest for a week, fasting in the forest, no food, little Water, and a Bear came up to where I had set up camp. I had a circle of Cedar around me. The Bear sensed the Medicine and simply put one claw on my leg, scratched a little, and then walked away. Good protection Medicine, that Cedar!" As the Medicine Man helped me create my protection ring, I thought about how many times Cedar has helped me.

I had an intense lupus flare many years ago, and my Grandfather told my Mother to gather Cedar and put the Medicine in my bath. It was then that I learned the power Cedar has to extract illness and heaviness from the body. I used this Plant in my healing sessions and Ceremonies to pull out all that needed clearing in the years to come. Aside from physical pain, such things as anger, resentment, fear, grief, and shame can impede the wholeness that we seek. With intention and vision, Cedar's Medicine can help us to acknowledge, feel, and release what has been waiting to go. It is deeply sacred to me, and I am so grateful for the healing properties it brings.

Cedar is an integral part of many of our Ceremonies. When we light this Medicine, it sparks and crackles, and this sound is said to call on our Spirit helpers. Cedar helps to protect and ground us. We place this Medicine in our moccasins so that we walk in a good way. We use Cedar in our sweat lodge and fasting Ceremonies to ward off negative energies. I have planted Cedar bushes around my home and hang Cedar in my doorways to keep the energy of my space clear.

Depending on where you live, Cedar might be a more plentiful and abundant Medicine than White Sage. Upon harvesting any Plant Medicine, I always thank Mother Earth for her gift and place something down for her in gratitude, like a Stone or another Plant. You can even sing her a song of thanks like I do.

Wiingashk (Sweetgrass)

I still remember the beautiful scent of Sweetgrass when I opened the cottage door. We would stay on the reserve every summer in this small yet cozy place on the Georgian Bay. These times would bring the excitement of using an outhouse, eating small boxes of sugary cereal, and taking refreshing swims in the most sacred Waters I know. Someone had burned the Sweetgrass Medicine, and the air still had remnants of its essence.

I can also remember my Grandparents' home smelling like this, remnants of Medicine, as though smudge had burned there. It seemed to be hidden, or at least that's how I remember it. This would make sense based on the generational trauma of my family, who had their Indigenous Medicine Ways colonized and stripped away. It wouldn't have felt safe to pass these teachings down, as there was trauma attached to both practicing and claiming Ceremony. Sadly, there were no formal instructions or "how to's." Generational trauma blocked that from happening. Instead, my child self began to learn how to absorb Medicine through memory, through scent, through how it made my heart feel. Sweetgrass does this: Its sweetness is purposeful; it pulls forward the memories that live deep inside, memories we thought were lost but we now reclaim.

Sweetgrass represents the hair of Mother Earth. When harvested, we braid it from the Earth, the Plant still attached to its roots. And like when we collect Cedar, we offer something back in gratitude. The three parts of the braid represent the body, mind, and Spirit—also, honesty, kindness, and love. This Medicine is added to our smudge to call on the good Spirits. I will often offer a braid of Sweetgrass to a friend, relative, or acquaintance as a gift of peace or forgiveness. When braided, it is often burned alone, its sweet scent filling spaces with beautiful energy.

Mashkodewashk (Sage)

One Christmas Eve, my Mother decided that we were not going to go to church. I was surprised, as we had always done this as part of our religious tradition. At the time, I didn't realize that she was trying to unlock herself from some of the colonial ways rooted inside our lineage. I see in retrospect that it was a beautiful act of reclamation that she made that day. We walked outside on the cold and quiet winter night and looked up at the Stars. She asked us to stand by the Cedar trees, and she lit some Sage. I could feel our Ancestors joining us, and it felt like a celebration, a coming home of sorts. As the Sage's scent aligned us back with our sacred ways, we remembered how to connect to Spirit outside the four walls of the church that the colonizers told us we needed. The blanket of snow on the Earth was our floor, the midnight-blue Sky flecked with Stars, our ceiling. A living and ever-present cathedral, and I realized how we had never needed walls.

Sage is the Medicine that most people know and love for the "smudge" Ceremony. Indigenous people typically use either White Sage or Desert Sage in their smudge. Desert sage carries potent medicinal characteristics as an astringent, antiseptic, and antifungal. It purifies the dense energies that we no longer need and helps to bring us back to a place of peace and connection. White sage is often used in our prayers and healing rituals and provides a way to connect to the Spirit World.

Wild White Sage is the Plant Medicine that receives the most attention when we speak of cultural appropriation as it has been popularized in New Age and spiritual communities. While some treat this Plant with the sacredness it deserves, others have commodified it and co-opted its original ceremonial use. It is now being overharvested and overconsumed. One of the challenges that this brings is the possibility that the original peoples who have centuries of connection to this Medicine will no longer have access to it.

After examining these issues of appropriation, overharvesting, and even taking your own journey within to discover the Plant Medicine of your Ancestors, if you choose to use White Sage, it is recommended that you take time to honor the Plant and know its source—or perhaps even grow your own. Suckerfish Moon calls us to purify what is not in alignment; therefore, we must walk with integrity. Honor the people whose teachings you're benefiting from by researching the history of the Indigenous people in your area. Make a gratitude offering to the Ancestors that held it in reverence. If you are harvesting it yourself, share with the Plant why you are using it and thank it. Developing a relationship with our Plant Kin deepens our level of respect in the actions that we take with any ritual or Ceremony.

Some alternatives to White Sage are:

- Rosemary
- Juniper
- Lavender
- Pine
- Spruce
- Bay Leaves
- Dandelion
- Calendula
- Mugwort
- Thyme
- Rose Petals

Medicine Reflection: What Plant Medicines on this list speak to you the most? Do you know what plants your Ancestors used? Are there any others that you would add?

Creating a relationship with Medicines from your lineage is a profound way of honoring yourself and the history of those from whom you learn. Building a relationship and learning about the Plant Medicines that speak to you for cleansing also shows respect to the traditional teachings that do not necessarily belong to you. So how do we do this? How do we reconnect to teachings that may have been lost or buried? For many of my students, building a relationship with their intuitive knowing, dream time, and inner wisdom has led them to find the plants that resonate with a part of their soul. The "Find Your Plant Ally" Ceremony described below is a place to start, and I hope that you may use it as a bridge to your knowing. The journey will help develop your relationship with the Plant world further and help you identify the plants that your Ancestors used as Medicine. Our Spirit always knows which Medicines we are meant to work with, and this journey will allow you to open up to receive what is in alignment with you.

MEDICINE JOURNEY
Find Your Plant Ally

Find a comfortable place to sit or lie down and begin to breathe. Tell your Ancestors that you will be retrieving a Plant that is a healing ally for you. As you continue to breathe, you see a bright golden door surrounded by Plants. As you walk through, you can smell the Medicines. They begin to enter your lungs, and you feel a sense of remembering.

There is so much beauty around you, and it feels lush and abundant. You come to a clearing on this path, and you see that your Ancestors are waiting for you. They take you by the hand and lead you to a Ceremony where they have gathered in a circle; as you enter, you feel seen and loved. Today they are practicing a cleansing and purification Ceremony, and they are using Plants that have spoken to them across the ages.

Smoke is rising, Medicines are crackling, and you are surrounded by the warmth and energy of all that is being done. You may have visions of a particular plant or hear names or see colors. Trust what you receive.

A Grandmother Spirit comes forward for you and places the Plant Medicine in your hands. As you feel the sensation on your palm, look down and see what she has offered you. She tells you that this Medicine speaks to your lineage somehow and that you can access it any time you may need it.

You ask her: *What is this plant called?*

As you listen, she speaks in some way that you can understand: a vision, words, or a knowing.

What is it used for?

Again, you listen for the guidance to reveal itself.

How can I best honor this Plant from this day forward?

And she delivers wisdom for you to use on your journey.

You turn to the rest of your Ancestors, and they come close to your space and commit to sharing their wisdom with you through your dream time, visions, meditations, and quiet time in nature. They remind you that when you are walking and particular plants call to you, communicate with them in your way. They are speaking to you for a reason. *You are the Medicine.* You take the Plant Medicine gift and hold it to your heart with gratitude.

Medicine Reflection: What Plant came forward for you on this journey? What guidance did you receive about this Plant?

SMOKE MEDICINE CEREMONY

This Ceremony can be used to cleanse your own body, mind, and Spirit, or those of your family or clients. Customize it with the Plant you may have received in the Plant Medicine journey. If you don't have access to that exact Plant, use one you are developing a relationship with; honor it with reverence.

1. **Open Sacred Space.**

   Open a window so that the energy has a place
   to go. However, if this isn't possible, trust that
   the Medicine is doing what it needs to do. Speak
   this prayer or one that resonates for you:

   *Dearest Creator, we ask you to hold and protect
   this space as we release what is no longer needed. I
   call to the East, the South, the West, the North, the
   Earth, the Sky to activate the Medicine we need for
   this cleanse. I call on my Ancestors, my Guides, and
   the highest loving energies to support and assist in
   this purification.*

2. **Light the Plant Medicine.**

   Traditionally, this is done with a match. Gently
   blow them out. Run your hands through the
   smoke before you start and send gratitude to
   the Medicines.

3. **As the Medicines smoke, use a tool to weave
   the smoke.**

   Use a feather or other fanning-type of tool—
   your hand will do, too—and weave the smoke
   around your body from the top of your head to
   the tips of your toes. Pay attention to the spaces
   under your arms, between your legs, and along
   the soles of your feet. Energy can get stuck
   there. If you are cleansing someone else, get
   them to turn around and do the back of their
   body as well.

   Important: If you are cleansing someone
   else, always ask permission to move the smoke
   around their body, especially if you are moving
   around sensitive parts.

Use your intuition as to where you need to concentrate. Sometimes the smoke will intensify around certain places of the body. The Medicine always knows.

Have the person (or yourself) feel what they are releasing or clearing out. The intention you set is vital during this Ceremony.

4. **Close the space and let the Medicine burn out.**

    Make sure it's out, dispose of the ashes into the Earth, and thank your Spirit helpers.

    Traditionally, we say a prayer when we do a smoke Ceremony for ourselves. Here is one that I use daily. Feel free to customize it for your own needs.

SMOKE MEDICINE PRAYER

May I cleanse my mind so that I may think uplifting thoughts.
May I cleanse my ears so that I may release any unkind words or energy that I have heard.
May I cleanse my mouth so that I may speak with love.
May I cleanse my throat so that I may speak the truth.
May I cleanse my heart of all that weighs heavy.
May I cleanse my center so that I may come back to trusting my inner wisdom.
I move this smoke down my body to help me root into Mother Earth and walk in a good way.
   Miigwetch (Thank you)

Frog Medicine Invocation

Dearest Frog, I invite you to continue uplifting my space with your cleansing Medicine. When the energy gets stagnant, I ask that you leap through my awareness so that I may clear out the clutter. Help to inform me whenever my body, mind, or Spirit needs purification. Your Medicine is now rooted in my awareness. I am blessed with your cleansing powers.

Namebine Giizis Moon Affirmation

I allow this purification Moon to bathe my sacred space and body with light and radiance. I am clear and aligned. I am the Medicine.

CHAPTER 6

WAAWAASKONE GIIZIS FLOWER MOON

Our fifth Moon of Creation is the time when the Plant world begins to come alive. It is in May when these beings showcase their life-giving nature and allow the world to see them in their fullest expression. During this time, we are asked to move our spiritual purpose into our body and walk the beauty way. We are encouraged to claim the Medicine we have come here with and step into our rising.

Moon Legend: How the Flowers Began to Bloom

In the early days, Creator planted many seeds. One by one, these seeds went into Aki, the Earth Mother. She held them with devotion and love and gathered each seed in her arms. The most magical thing about each seed was that they held their own Medicine gifts. Each one carried certain qualities that made them a little bit different from their neighboring seed. Each seed was coded with a unique wisdom expression, aligned with enormous potential.

The seeds would cuddle into the warm, nourishing Soil that Mother Earth provided. They felt safe and cozy in their seed state, protected from the elements, sheltered from the storms. Days went by, and the seeds remained seeds. Some of the seeds began to wonder if there was anything more to life than staying small and comfortable. They felt this deep calling in their hearts, a longing to grow and evolve, but they didn't know the next step.

One morning, the Sunflower seed awoke after dreaming. "I just had a dream where I was this bold, tall flower. My face looked up to Grandfather Sun, and I was beautiful and vibrant yellow!" The others listened with excitement. Rose seed chimed in and said they had been having visions of their heart expanding in similar ways. The Tulip seeds admitted that they, too, were feeling inner stirrings of something new, something different. After sharing, they all decided that they would gather their courage to take a new journey. They had always been curious about what was beyond their comfortable space but had never ventured out. They started to plan to take their journey upward through the Soil. Some other seeds heard of their plan, and some decided they wanted to venture out, too. Others were quite comfortable staying where they were and shared that they were too afraid of the dangers that might be above.

The next day, the journey began. It was more difficult than expected, with twists and turns along the way. There was no clear path and nobody to guide the way. At times the rains would wash down, and they would fall behind. At other times, they would get thrown around by an animal digging. Many times, they felt discouraged and almost gave up. Every day they built resilience from their struggle, and every day, they rooted down into trust that they were on the right path.

One morning, after journeying all night long, they saw a source of light. They all began to shoot toward it with hope and anticipation, and lo and behold, Grandfather Sun was there to meet them, radiating and illuminating their warmth, heat, and love. The seeds reached toward Sun, and the most magical thing began to happen. Their shells began to crack open, and bit by bit, the tiniest hints of color and vibrancy began to show through. After moving through so much discomfort, the seeds were happy to feel wrapped in safety again. They happily rooted themselves into a spot where they could easily enjoy the sunshine, the rain, and the wind. They celebrated each other as, one by one, the seedlings blossomed into beautiful flowers.

The flowers acknowledged how far they had come. As they looked back on their journey, they saw that their determination, trust, and heartfelt courage led them to their brilliant becoming. They were so grateful that they had listened to their inner voices and calling, for they were now able to rise into who they were meant to be.

Animal Spirit: *Memengwaa* (Butterfly)

The Animal Spirit that best represents the fourth Moon is Butterfly, or as they are known in Anishiinabemowin, *Memengwaa*. With its brilliant Medicine of transformation, rebirth, and flight, Butterfly moves through this Moon phase to teach us that we gain resilience, wisdom, and renewed courage through our struggles. Caterpillar trusts in the vision of its Medicine and potential. They carry a unique wisdom expression that one day informs their transformation into a winged creature. This Moon asks us to reflect on our journeys and see how the struggles and challenges have helped guide our path. These times in our lives are the moments when we evolve deeply, stepping into chrysalises of change. These are the moments when we dissolve the parts that are no longer aligned to become more of who we are meant to be, just as Caterpillar's body must be dissolved to realize their greatest potential in the form of Butterfly.

Butterfly Message

- You can transform challenges into beauty.
- You are naturally gifted with wings to soar.
- Dissolving old ways leads to new magic.
- As in our Creation stories, beauty is birthed from change.

A LIFE OF PURPOSE

What is my purpose? What is my true calling? As humans, we have long been conditioned to look outside ourselves for the answers to these questions. We have been taught that the internal wisdom guiding us is not something we can trust. We give our power away, to leaders, to partners, to friends, to bosses. We are told by advertising and social media that we are not good enough and need to be fixed, and we believe it. We are bombarded by societal messages that we must strive, achieve, and reach this imaginary status of perfection before we can finally accept ourselves. It blinds us to the Medicine we all carry inside us.

My clients often have this vision of finally "making it" to their purpose. These visions are grand and beautiful: meeting Oprah, traveling the world as a famous speaker, working remotely from the beach as a digital nomad. Dreaming big is essential. But it takes time for big dreams to manifest and, in the meantime, so many of us begin to feel that the way we are living *now* is somehow not enough, that *we* are not enough. The Flower Moon guides us to our becoming and reminds us that we are blossoming at the pace that is correct for us.

I know people who walk into a room and instantly brighten it with their smiles. I am personally inspired by natural storytellers who share their truth authentically. I know folks whose mere presence brings light to others simply by being true to who they are. My youngest son giggles, and our home fills with joy, while my oldest son will share observations that the rest of us do not see. I have a friend whose cooking is filled with so much love that every bite feels healing. These are simple gifts, but they change my life regularly.

Owning your Medicine and sharing it doesn't have to be complicated. It's the most uncomplicated thing in the world, because it is something you have always walked with. It's a burst of energy that has always flowed through you. This energetic signature combines your natural frequency, lived experience, and deep Ancestral knowing you've held for lifetimes.

So, how do we go about finding that brilliant Medicine that is ours alone? Our journey through life's challenges can often reveal aspects of ourselves that have been waiting to be birthed. Sometimes the depth of our Medicine can be found through pain. This has been the case in my life journey with my physical health. Each flare-up or setback led me to discover the deep Medicine that flowed through my blood and bones. As I healed myself, I connected to the Ancestral wisdom colonization had closed off to me. Now, I see that every flare-up of lupus has taken me to the next level of transformation.

Moving through chronic pain has taught me the power of resilience, compassion, and self-love. I have held space for thousands in their suffering because I deeply know what it feels like to hurt. Every step of transmuting my pain into droplets of light has become an ocean of healing for others. You, too, can rise from the ashes. We all can.

This painful, unsettling, transformative part of finding our Medicine is reflected in the chrysalis phase of Caterpillar's journey. When transformation begins, the chrysalis form breaks down and turns to mush. The breakdown of the chrysalis mirrors our life challenges, that time when everything feels uncertain and impossible—when *everything* falls apart.

But not everything is gone. During the transformation of Caterpillar into Butterfly, they hold on to their imaginal cells. These latent cells are a blueprint for what they are to become—Butterfly's essential nature. Even when they are a mass of goo, Butterfly knows that they will fly one day. And our souls know, too. That's what our Medicine is: imaginal cells that understand who we are, even when we don't. This knowledge has been with us since birth. It isn't going anywhere, even as we break down.

Coming back to the truth of our Medicine and the positive impact our presence can have in the world takes healing, commitment, and trust. We must bring awareness to how the world has impacted us and then bring healing to these pieces of us waiting to be acknowledged and loved. And we must do this by caring for our pain, finding support—in therapy, energy work, or community—and offering love to our perfectly imperfect selves. The beautiful wisdom that comes from walking this healing journey through the goo becomes a rooted part of who we are and allows us to serve others with empathy. I like to call that "Soul Gold."

Medicine Reflection: What are the struggles or challenges you have gone through in your life that have cracked open aspects of your Medicine? What is your "Soul Gold"?

MEDICINE JOURNEY
Soul Gold Retrieval

Find a comfortable place to sit or lie down, and begin to breathe. Call on the Butterfly Spirit to lead you through your transformation. As you begin, envision yourself as a caterpillar; you'll see a bright golden door surrounded by rainbow light. As you open the door and move through, you feel yourself surrounded by a warm cocoon.

In this cocoon, a vision or memory of one of the most challenging events in your life comes forward. You are safe and protected here; there is nothing to fear. As you remember, you begin to unravel, dissolve, and fall apart. There is a sense of disorientation as you turn into goo.

In this state of goo, you carry a set of incredible magical cells. They contain the Soul Gold that has always been a part of you. Even when you feel like everything around you is dissolving, these cells hold the vision of who you are. The wind begins to blow around you, and there is an activation that happens. Your Soul Gold is gathered from the path you have walked, the wisdom that you have gained from this lifetime and beyond, and you begin to emerge into a new state of being. Grandfather Sun begins to radiate powerfully over your body, and you are remade with wings.

Slowly and gently, you spread those wings and begin to flap them. Soar with your Soul Gold activated and feel the lightness, the connection, and the spark of your divinity realign with your energy. Your Soul Gold begins to flow out of every pore of your skin. You are radiant. *You are the Medicine.*

Gently float back down to Earth, back to your path, standing taller and more rooted in all that you are. The journey is complete. Move through the door, breathe yourself back into your space, and at your own pace and time, come back into your room and open your eyes.

REMEMBERING THE CHILD WITHIN

Struggles or challenges are not the only way that we can access our Medicine gifts. One way of accessing our Medicine is to go back and explore the gifts of your child self. When I was little, my abilities as a seer and empath were revealed. My Ancestors would visit me at night through visions, and my dreams were filled with vibrant healing journeys and messages. In my waking life, I would go into a room and feel people's emotions—even if their faces or words were closed doors, revealing nothing. My mother and Grandfather would speak about how I was a seer and a visionary. My grandparents would discuss on which side of the family line my gifts originated. My eldest son holds similar gifts.

I'm grateful I had a mother who saw me, held space for me, and helped nurture these parts of me. I would wake in the morning and tell her about what I had "imagined" the night before. Speaking of our Dreamtime was a regular morning conversation. To this day, I fly and visit and offer healings in my Dreamtime. It always leaves me in awe when people tell me I visited them and offered them Medicine/Ceremony or I dream of homeopathic remedies that certain people may need. My mother kept my sensitive heart safe, advocating for me in school when teachers said I was too quiet. She put me in dance and piano so that I could find ways to express myself. She shared stories about her childhood, too, and I saw that we were similar. This sharing helped me to see my own Medicine. To this day, when I remember these aspects of my child self or stories from my past, it reminds me of my Medicine, and it can do the same for you.

Medicine Reflection: As a child, what did you want to be when you "grew up"? What lit up your heart?

WHAT COMES WITH EASE?

Another way to access your unique Medicine is to reflect on what is easy for you to do. Your Medicine doesn't have to be complicated. You've probably been connecting with aspects of it for as long as you've been alive. They may not seem magnificent or special to you, but your natural gifts and energy could be life changing for someone else.

For as long as I can remember, people have opened up to me. When I was a teenager, I worked in a jewelry store and customers would come in and tell me their life stories and share their problems without a word from me. I went through hundreds of tissue boxes in my private practice, as my clients would sit before me and the tears would inevitably flow. I would hear these words often: "I haven't cried in years!" or "I don't know what's wrong with me—I cry every time I'm here!"

What I came to know after these experiences is that being a space holder is part of my natural Medicine. People instantly feel safe, seen, and held. It's not something I force, manifest, or create. I have simply learned to allow what is natural to me to flow through me, and as a result, thousands of people have been moved toward healing. Take a moment to reflect on this for yourself. What flows from you effortlessly, without you having to try too hard? Flower Moon encourages us to see how we bloom in many moments throughout our days; sometimes what seems insignificant is the most important.

An Indigenous Elder once shared this with me: "Every human's purpose in this lifetime is to raise the consciousness of this planet and help it evolve to a greater state of love." I loved this wisdom. How do we help the Earth evolve to a greater state of love? We do this through engaging in our healing work and focusing on how our soul is calling us to share our gifts. We then take action in the ways we are guided. Some days that might be a smile; some days, it might be a healing touch. Simple things can have a considerable impact.

One of my dear friends radiates sunshine everywhere she goes. People's hearts instantly open when she is around. When my son was a baby, she came to visit, and when she said hello, he started to blink his eyes in amazement and awe. Her sparkly nature seems effortless for her to live by each and every day. Her presence is something she has carried with her for her entire life, and there is no doubt in my mind that she will continue to illuminate the world in this way until her last breath. It's not complicated. She hasn't had to take a million courses to be proficient in her sunshine. She just lives it, owns it, and the world is a better place because of it.

My friend has done a lot of healing work in her life to walk confidently in her Medicine. Others have tried to dim her light or have walked away from it, but my friend has worked hard to keep walking, loving, and accepting herself precisely as she is. It's not always an easy path to remain rooted in who you are. People will judge you, feel jealous of you, or even leave your life. It can be difficult to accept this as people often see it as overconfidence when you love yourself. Let that go—it's not your pain. Bless them, and then walk toward your warm embrace of self-love. The rewards will far outweigh the risks, as your job here on this Earth is to keep being you in all your magnificence.

An astrologer once told me that the Sun doesn't care who it shines on. It doesn't care if it burns you; it just shines. I love this reminder to keep doing our thing and being who we are. Your Medicine presence changes lives. It only takes one voice to impact millions. It only takes one presence to inspire many.

Medicine Reflection: What qualities seem to flow effortlessly from you? What compliments do you get the most often?

RISE

Some of the most beautiful moments of my career have been witnessing folks rising. I've seen women leave their abusive partners or finally speak a truth that has been making them sick for years. I've seen women change careers and start businesses that make a huge impact in the world. I've seen women share their voices as activists and Healers, and musicians, artists, and authors. I've seen so much magic in their journeys.

What I know to be true is that our lived experience guides and informs our Medicine deeply. The challenges we move through, the lows, the highs, the sadness, the joy— it's all wisdom gained from our journey. It all becomes the Medicine we are meant to live. The most powerful claiming of Soul Gold I have witnessed in my life has been women who leave their abusive partners, root into their worthiness, and step into being leaders of self-love. Folks who live with chronic illness find their healer within and teach others to find theirs. People who had an abusive childhood decide to change that cycle and become the most nurturing and supportive parents. Claiming your Soul Gold is a beautiful result of being conscious and doing your healing work. The journey from challenge to beauty requires dedication and perseverance. And in my experience, it's worth it.

I will never forget a client I served five years ago named Mae who had been dealing with chronic pain for some time. When she sat in front of me, I instantly felt her beauty and light. When she spoke, love seemed to flow into every corner of my room. She had charisma and sparkle, was full of gratitude and grace, and I instantly felt that she cared deeply about everyone who crossed her path. I also noticed that she couldn't see it as I did. A part of her was blind to her magic. All she saw and felt was her own pain.

Then she attended one of my mentorship weekends. This was a big step for her because she didn't tend to step out of her comfort zone often—especially if doing so required her to be visible. At these weekends I offered every attendee five minutes to demonstrate their Medicine. When it was Mae's turn, she stood up tall and was suddenly transformed. She was a tiny woman who I knew felt restricted by pain, but in the moments that followed, an angelic singing voice flowed out of her. A tremendous voice! I was blown away. She sang opera, and every person in the room listened with rapt attention. At the end of her song, we were all in tears. It had only been three minutes, but she changed my life and the lives of everyone in that room. We saw in Mae that anyone can contain multitudes of breathtaking gifts. Beauty and talent reside in us all.

Mae had kept this part of her Medicine hidden and oppressed for various reasons: family wounds, self-doubt, fear of judgment. But she did the work to heal through the layers of her life, starting that weekend. She remembered what lit up her soul, she reclaimed her natural gifts, and she made a conscious decision to rise. She transformed her pain and doubt into blessings and gratitude. Today, Mae has a thriving business singing at formal events and is flourishing in her Spirit and her body.

You don't need to be a secret opera singer like Mae, but this story illustrates how we can all transform our pain into beauty and love that can fill our world. Our voice, our presence, our heart can be enough.

Medicine Reflection: After reflection on these teachings, what do you feel your Medicine is?

Butterfly Medicine Invocation

Dearest Butterfly, I invite you to remind me of the power of dissolving and unwinding. It's safe to let go in order to become. Remind me of the power that the cocoon holds. May I remember that my wings have always been waiting for me and that transformation is an essential part of my flight. I am grateful for your reminders that beauty lives within me through all of the layers of my process. As I remember and reclaim all of myself, I spread my wings and take flight toward all that I am becoming.

Waawaaskone Giizis Moon Affirmation

As I reconnect and remember that my gifts are profound, I open my Spirit to the light of Creation. I am fully ready to blossom and shine. I am the Medicine.

CHAPTER 7

ODE'MIIN GIIZIS
STRAWBERRY MOON

Our sixth Moon of Creation is said to be the time when we should welcome everyone into our hearts, regardless of any disagreements or challenges. It was a time of the yearly feast in June, where we honored reconciliation and coming together. During this time, we let go of judging another, and we practice humility, seeing the humanity of all of our Kin. This is the time that we are reminded of what true love is and what that looks like in our actions. The Strawberry ripens during this cycle, and we call it the "heart berry" due to its shape and Medicine for the body.

MOON LEGEND: HOW STRAWBERRY
BECAME THE HEART BERRY

In the beginning, Creator was inspired to create diversity and alignment within those Plants and Trees that bore fruit. Creator dreamed up many different flavors, colors, and nutrients, excited to splash the Earth with beauty.

As each new Plant or Tree came into being, they began to notice their differences. When they spoke to each other, they started to see that they had differing opinions about how to grow in the best way or how to create the best fruit. They started to judge one another's appearances and put one another down. They began to criticize and attack one another. Hearts were broken, Spirits were damaged, and harm was done.

There was a great divide on the Earth. A lack of understanding and a split began to separate the Plants and Trees into groups. Some groups felt that they were better than the others because there were more of them. Other groups marched through Land that they had never inhabited because they felt entitled to take up that space. There was destruction and fighting, and Creator decided that something must be done! They decided to dream something new into being, something that would bring love to the chaos. That night, Creator had a profound dream of a brilliant red berry. It carried its seeds on the outside and was shaped like a heart. When ripe, this fruit brought great sweetness. The name of it was the Strawberry—*Ode'miin*.

Creator decided to plant this Medicine all around the Trees and Plants and told the birds to begin sharing and carrying Strawberry to all of the places they visit. As they did this, a magical thing happened. The Medicine of Strawberry started to impact everyone they met. There was a greater sense of love and acceptance that started to flow through all the Forests and Earth space. All of Creation began to see each other at the heart level. Since many of them had done harm, they started offering their fruit as a gift of reparation to their Kin. They gathered to help those who were smaller or sick. They committed to speaking up when someone gossiped or shamed another. They leaned back and listened to the stories of one another. They made repairs where they had abused or oppressed. They healed—all because of Strawberry. And from that day forward, it was known as the Heart berry, the one that helps us move love into action.

Animal Spirit: Nika (Canada Goose)

The Animal Spirit that best represents our Sixth Moon is Canada Goose—or *Nika,* as they are known in Anishiinabemowin—with their Medicine of community, leadership, cooperation, allyship, and the sacred circle. Canada Goose moves with us through this Moon phase to remind us that the best way to move through life is with teamwork. We never leave behind those who are weak or sick; we stand behind them and support them along the journey. Canada Goose teaches us about fellowship and kinship. They ask us to lean on each other when needed and to take turns in leadership roles. Everyone is honored with loyalty and devotion in the sacred circle, according to Canada Goose Spirit. It teaches us that you belong, no matter who you are. We open our hearts, we practice uplifting those who need it, and we remember that we can fly farther together.

Canada Goose Message

- We cannot fly free unless we all fly free.
- We uplift and help those who are in need.
- Our actions create equal reactions—be mindful.
- True oneness comes from seeing the truth of another's reality.

THE MEDICINE OF A CIRCLE

The circle describes many aspects of the physical world and our Relations, giving it deep meaning to Indigenous people. From the shape of the Celestial beings of the Sun, Moon, Planets, and Stars, to the intricate weavings of bird nests, spiderwebs, or drops rippling in Water, the circle is reflected in much of our sacred world. The cyclical nature of our seasons, the Moon cycles, and our life cycles all move in circles. Circle Medicine reminds us that we are all connected. If harm occurs to one of our Relations, it happens to us all. In this way of seeing the world, every action creates a ripple of reaction. We ask ourselves, *How do we maintain harmony with all of our Kin? How do we come back into balance?*

> **Medicine Reflection:** What abuse, harm, and violence do you witness in our world?

During this month, in the Northern Hemisphere, we celebrate the Summer Solstice. In our country, we also celebrate National Indigenous People's Day. It's my favorite time to participate in Ceremony. For the last 15 years, I have hosted a Summer Solstice Circle, with our Ancestors filling the room, our Guides informing us, and Creator protecting the space. It always feels like a powerful portal, as we celebrate Grandfather Sun in his brightest light. It always feels like a space where I am coming home.

Our Elders teach us that when we sit in circle, nobody is better or less than another. The intention is that we create equity in this space, seeing each other in our wholeness. In circle, we are all Healers, teachers, wisdom and Medicine keepers. We also hold space for our wounds, trauma, and triggers. When we sit in this living, breathing, alchemic space, we are able to see each other in our true humanity. During these Ceremonies, I offer a bowl of strawberries, the heart berry. It is my intention as we bless this Medicine and take it into our bodies that we are able to listen to each other's lived experience, hold each other in a sacred way, and uplift those who may need our help. The circle is a place where we can mend differences and understand each other. Circle Medicine brings profound wholeness, community, and love.

"WE ARE ALL ONE"

One with the Waters and the Land. One with the Animals and the Stars. From an Indigenous perspective, we see through the lens of oneness to describe our interconnected relationship with all beings. It is part of who I am, imbued in my bones and Spirit, and this is a beautiful and sacred truth from an Indigenous worldview. I hold this sentiment and teaching close to my heart and have had many moments of feeling "oneness." However, this meaning of oneness assumes that all people are moving with humility, reciprocity, and truth. In our current world, this includes honoring the differences in another's experience and the injustice and inequity that BIPOC experience. Sadly, this teaching has been twisted and overused in our spiritual and New Age communities, erasing the real and lived experiences of BIPOC folks.

Using the phrase "We are all One" can cause harm, and as Yoga Unity Activist Susanna Barkataki says in her book *Embrace Yoga's Roots*, "To get to true oneness, we have to face the ways we may have been complicit in causing separation." She further explains that this statement doesn't acknowledge privilege, racial bias, or the power imbalances that exist in our world. As an Indigenous Woman, I have walked in the truth of oneness with my Kin and have also experienced oppression, marginalization, and racism, which tells me that I am separate. In the last couple of years, I have started to reflect on how to bridge these two truths and what my role is in walking this in the world. My vision holds carrying the Strawberry Moon Medicine, walking the depth of love that I have for all beings into action. To deepen this practice, I commit to dismantling my own privilege and inherent bias daily, as I believe that we all need to do this work.

> **Medicine Reflection:** Do you use the phrase "We are all One"? What changes might you make as a result of knowing that it can be harmful?

How to Appreciate, Not Appropriate

In Chapter 6, we spoke about appropriation with regard to Plant Medicines, specifically the Ceremony of smudging and the use of white sage. Here is some other wisdom that you may want to consider.

1. *Investigate your motivations.*

   What is your intention when you use drums, smudge, and feathers—your social media posts and marketing? Are you trying to use them to gain followers or boost your popularity? Do you have a relationship with these ceremonial, sacred objects? Are you praying to them and honoring them daily or simply using them to look the part?

2. *Know the history.*

The Indian Act, which was passed in 1876, explicitly banned and outlawed the practice of our Medicines until 1951, and it wasn't until 1996 that it was agreed that this portion of the act was oppressive. We work so hard every day to reclaim what has been taken away from us. Hold these facts in your heart, root down into the truth, and allow yourself to be guided from there.

3. *Admire and celebrate authentically.*

Wear your moccasins, mukluks, and beaded earrings. Buy Indigenous artwork, carvings, creations, and Dreamcatchers. Our culture has so much magnificence to love. Support and buy from Indigenous people or companies. Ask them if they are willing to share a teaching or story with you about their Medicine so that you can honor this daily.

4. *Acknowledge the present-day reality.*

Can you acknowledge and hold both the light and the dark of our country? If you are taking Medicines to use for your own profit, are you acknowledging the effects that the lack of clean Water, the missing and murdered Indigenous and Two-Spirit folks, the generational trauma that residential schools caused and that attempted genocide has had on our people? Suicide, alcohol abuse, violent deaths, racism. It all exists here and now.

5. *Support Indigenous voices.*

    Taking from an oppressed group without
    acknowledging what they go through to share
    their Medicines is not in right relation. Are you
    learning from Indigenous people? If so, how
    can you support their offerings, their words,
    their Medicine. Share their voice, amplify their
    words, and pay them for their labor. For so many
    years, the majority of authors and influencers
    in the Spiritual and New Age realm have been
    white women. Many of them are profiting and
    making money off our teachings. Help us to rise,
    too! I am envisioning a world where Indigenous
    Healers, Teachers, and Authors are invited
    equitably. How can you support this vision?

6. *Be respectful of the term "Spirit Animal."*

    It does not refer to your friend, a celebrity, or
    your favorite food. Animal Spirits are sacred to
    our people. They are our relatives, Ancestors,
    guardians, siblings, friends. To use that term
    jokingly is harmful. My community is filled
    with many non-Indigenous people who have
    learned how to honor them as deeply sacred
    beings. You can, too.

7. *Never wear a Headdress.*

    A Headdress is a very sacred item and does not
    belong in your next photoshoot. A Headdress
    is offered to someone in the community,
    usually a leader, as a gift. They must go through
    Ceremonies and protocols to receive one. There
    are responsibilities that go along with wearing
    a Headdress; it carries potent and sacred energy.

Please don't wear it to the next outdoor music festival you go to.

8. ***Research your own ancestry.***

I guarantee that if you feel drawn to Indigenous teachings, your Ancestors most likely practiced beautiful Ceremonies and rituals. Research where your Ancestors are from and what Ceremonies and rituals they used. Open your heart, Spirit, and mind, and let your Ancestors teach you. There is so much remembering in your blood and bones waiting to be uncovered. I believe that we are all on a journey of reconnection and reclaiming. We will dive deeper into this in a future chapter.

9. ***Bring everything back to the sacred.***

This means something different to everyone. However, honoring the fullness of a Ceremony, an item, a Medicine tool, or anything else on your spiritual tool belt is an important practice. Find your way, listen to your heart, and let Spirit guide you to the next right step.

After receiving so many varying responses to my words on this topic, I realized how hard it is to be compassionate with ourselves when we think we may have harmed or hurt someone. Many times, we jump to defensiveness or shut down completely. I understand. It hasn't always been safe to mess up and make mistakes. I believe the antidote to defensiveness or shutdown is compassion for self. If we can keep our hearts open, as Strawberry Moon guides us to do, we can make repair. Repair is the Medicine that heals cracks and brings us back together. It's a Medicine that we all need at this time in the world.

MEDICINE JOURNEY
Collective Repair

Plant your feet firmly upon the floor, and envision the Earth securely holding you. Take a moment to place your hands upon your heart and remind yourself that you are safe to feel all that is rising within. Offer yourself compassion for anything you didn't know before or the mistakes you may have made. We now call on the Canada Goose to surround us with divine healing. Envision hundreds of beautiful birds flapping their enormous wings around you; they lift any shame, blame, or other emotions that need to go.

A Medicine Person steps forward, holding a Goose feather in their hands; they place this over your heart center and ask:

Where might you have unknowingly caused harm with your practices? Let anything that you may have pushed down rise. Feel your hands on your heart and speak your intention to make repair.

What do you now know that you didn't before? Let anything rise that you did not have a deeper understanding of. Feel your hands on your heart and speak your intention to make repair.

The wind picks up all around you and swirls you into a sacred circle filled with all Guides, teachings, Medicines, Ceremonies, tools, and rituals that you carry in your mind and heart. How can you make repairs today in your life and in the lives of those you love and care about? Is there any repair that you need to make in your communities and beyond? Set this intention and send it to the Geese. They take this and offer uplifting and healing energy to all who need it today. *You are the Medicine.*

Come back to your body, hands on your heart, and make a commitment for how you will journey this into the world.

If you have come to help me, you are wasting your time.
If you have come because your liberation is bound
up with mine, then let us work together.

— LILLA WATSON, ABORIGINAL WISDOM KEEPER

ALLIES AND ACCOMPLICES

An ally in social justice spaces is defined as someone from a dominant or majority group who is working to end oppression by supporting marginalized communities. They acknowledge that they carry privilege and power that they can use to educate others while also doing their own inequity and injustice work. An accomplice, however, is defined as someone who takes steps to disrupt the harmful narrative of white supremacy while actively seeking solutions and acting on them, even if that means they lose social or other types of status or different levels of prestige. I have many allies and accomplices in my communities, and I am grateful for both.

From a personal level, I can share the difference in how I've experienced those who walk in allyship, and those who step forward as an accomplice. An ally will read articles I have shared and then share about what they are learning. They will buy Dreamcatchers, Medicines, and artwork from Indigenous creators, support their businesses, uplift their voices, and share their gifts. An accomplice moves into even more action. Accomplices get involved in the communities I share about, helping to raise money and offer support. They will put their own comfort on the line to assist those who don't have their basic needs met, giving up time, resources, or positions of power. The accomplices in my communities engage in conscious reflection, anti-racism work, and reciprocity often. Many in my community have become vocal supporters for my people. I can see how part of my purpose is to build diverse and inclusive communities of folks who journey with me to uncover the truth and move toward reconciliation together. The communities I build connect them to their own Medicine, so instead of seeking and taking, they give back.

They share the truth of those who have never had a voice, and they educate themselves to see the impact of racism against Indigenous people in our country. They have opened their hearts to listen without getting defensive; they have uplifted Black, Brown, and Indigenous voices; and they have looked at the ways they may be contributing to harm through appropriation, inherent biases, and their privilege.

I am deeply grateful for the allies and accomplices that travel with me on this journey, for many have crossed my path over the two decades of my work in the world. There are so many folks in my communities that uplift, support, donate, share, and help. I am so grateful for those who walk in right relationship and reciprocity. Building and nurturing these relationships is what I'm here for, and what I show up for. I am so honored to navigate this life with you. We need all of us. The ones who march, support, tend, heal, donate. Activism shows up in many forms. Keep going. You never know what seeds you may be planting and change you may be making.

Brave Spaces

A few years ago, I took a diversity and inclusion course with facilitators Desiree Adaway and Ericka Hines from the Adaway Group around building inclusive spaces. On our first call, they shared that our time together wouldn't be a safe space—it would be a brave space. When they shared these words, I got chills. For so long, I have seen teachers, facilitators, and Guides share that they hold safe space, but

I had never heard of a brave space. My experience in this brave space was that we were "humble and ready to fumble," as Ericka wisely shared. We made mistakes, we asked questions that felt uncomfortable, we examined our biases, and we dismantled and broke down the walls we had become accustomed to. We explored a more accurate meaning of equity and discussed how we can walk toward this in imperfect ways. I felt exposed and vulnerable but examined all the ways I had been complicit. But it was life changing. I left that space feeling like I had learned that sometimes "safe" spaces meant that we bypassed the most important topics that we need to be looking at. I left that brave space feeling free to make mistakes, learn, fall, and try again. I committed to creating brave spaces from that day forward, even if that meant that I would lose people in the process. I wanted to be an accomplice for change.

> **Medicine Reflection:** In what ways are the spaces you occupy safe spaces? Where are the brave spaces? What is the difference?

Canada Goose Medicine Invocation

Dearest Canada Goose, I invite you to help me stay rooted in my heart and open it to liberation for all. Help me to see that all my Relations are worthy of my love and care. Remind me what true community and brave spaces look like. I am open to listening and learning about ways that I can do better. Continue to show me the vision of a world where there is equity and harmony for all. Help me to move this love into action every single day.

Ode'miin Giizis Moon Affirmation

As I remember the power that my heart holds to make amends and repair harm, I contribute to the well-being and healing of all of my Relations. I am the Medicine.

CHAPTER 8

MSKOMINI GIIZIS
RASPBERRY MOON

Our seventh Moon of Creation is said to be a time where we move through the thorns of life to get to the fruit. It is in the month of July when we see that change is necessary, and cycles of hardship and trauma can be broken. The Raspberry is a delicate fruit when harvested, but when treated with kindness, it flourishes. This Moon teaches us that we can shift the impacts of harshness over time with tenderness. When we do this, we create ripples that touch those around us and the generations to come.

Moon Legend: How the Raspberry Came to Be

A shift was happening on Mother Earth. There was new energy of power and domination coming from the East. If you listened closely, you could hear voices speaking of the plans and intentions to strip love away and make sure everyone was the same. A controlling spirit had taken over the Earth; things were out of balance, and fear was amplifying.

Everyone found themselves huddling together, worried about these seemingly powerful energies. One night, this force came to the place where the berries grew. They looked the berries up and down, judging their appearances and differences. Strawberry, Blackberry, and Blueberry all passed their inspection. At this time, Raspberry was all thorns and, as they were very young, they had not yet learned how to grow fruit. The forces came and were appalled about their lack of fruit. "You need to be like the others!" they said. "We are taking all the young Raspberry bushes to strip away all that is not good about you and show you how to be in the world."

As the young Raspberries were separated from their Elders and parents, their hearts broke. They were placed in a tiny spot of Land where there was little Water and sunlight. All that was familiar to them was taken away. The Soil was drier than they were used to and the Water less plentiful. These young plants missed their families and the love that once surrounded them. They lost connection to their Spirit, their purpose, and their life force. Sadly, they had lost their reason for growing.

One day, Grandfather Sun heard that this was happening and set up a plan to bring them back home. Sun told the controlling spirits to release the Raspberry. The spirits agreed, for they had accomplished their mission. When the Sun reached Raspberry, Grandfather saw how broken and fragile the Raspberries were. Sun infused them with light, warmth, and love and welcomed them back where they were meant to be.

Raspberry grew and had children. These children had their own children, and those children had their own children. With each generation, the Ancestors of the past were remembered and honored for all that they had endured. Sometimes, the children would have the odd dream or vision of trauma of the past, the memories still in their cells. Luckily, their Ancestors had also passed on resilience and wisdom. With each generation, Spirits began to heal, especially when kindness and gentleness were shown.

Raspberry would dream of their old ways of knowing, visions reminding them of where they came from and who they were. Bit by bit, they reclaimed their identity, standing in pride. One day, after being fed with lots of sunlight, fresh Water, and love, Raspberry sprouted the beautiful berry that we know today. They kept parts of their fragile nature to remind all who handled them about the importance of tender care. Their lineage had moved through much hardship and trauma, but they learned how to walk through the thorns, find wisdom, and become the fruit they were meant to be.

Animal Spirit: *Gaag* (Porcupine)

The Animal Spirit that best represents our Seventh Moon is Porcupine or, as they are known in Anishiinabemowin, *Gaag*, with its Medicine that reminds us to free ourselves from guilt and shame. Porcupine calls us back to the beauty of the innocence we carried as a child. The prickles or thorns that our Ancestors experienced may still reside in our energy, but with each generation, the trauma can move into healing. Traditionally, Indigenous people have used Porcupine quills to create and adorn gorgeous sweetgrass baskets, earrings, and other works of art—an example of how one can transmute something that might seem harsh or sharp into beauty.

Porcupine Message

- Be curious about the wisdom available to you.
- Holding on to shame and guilt doesn't serve you.

- Healing through generational harm is possible.
- You are worthy of reclaiming your divine, innocent nature.

THE PAIN OF COLONIZATION

When the school is on the reserve, the child lives with its parents, who are savages, and though he may learn to read and write, his habits and training mode of thought are Indian. He is simply a savage who can read and write. . . . Indian children should be withdrawn as much as possible from the parental influence. . . put them in central training industrial schools where they will acquire the habits and modes of thought of white men.

— PRIME MINISTER JOHN A. MACDONALD, 1879

Like the Raspberries who were taken from all that was familiar, my maternal Grandparents and paternal Grandmother went to residential school in Spanish, Ontario, Canada. There are heartbreaking stories of what happened in residential schools across our country. A Truth and Reconciliation Commission report documented 37,951 claims made for injuries resulting from physical and sexual abuse in residential schools. Additionally, 3,200 children were recorded to have died, with many estimating the numbers to be much higher. At the beginning of this book, I referenced mass grave sites recently "found" on the grounds of residential schools. Canadians are outraged and shocked, but we have been living with the truth and pain all along. I have been speaking about these tragedies for years and only now are other people starting to see them. My call to action is that you read the full report by the Truth and Reconciliation Commission—see the endnotes.

Due to colonization, residential school, and the attempted genocide of Indigenous people, the reclamation of our Medicine ways, language, foods, and traditional knowledge has been challenging. In his book *Unreconciled*, Jesse Wente speaks about the direct impact of residential schools on him and his family. In reflecting on the effects of the trauma, he shares that he and his family were the "exact kind of Indian they had hoped to produce." His Grandmother attended the same school as my Grandparents and when I read these words, I got chills and felt the layers of shame that I carry. His words reminded me that it's not my fault I have not felt enough as I am. It was designed to be that way.

It has been a journey to retrieve things in a healed way and restore harmony where trauma lives. Indigenous people were shamed, beaten down, and punished for using our Medicine gifts, language, and traditions. Often, Medicine People had to practice in secret and, as we discussed in earlier chapters, some of our Ceremonies were outlawed or banned. Residential school tried to scrub the "Indian out of the child." The intentions to assimilate and colonize worked with devastating consequences. Those layers of grief and shame that continue to rise for me around this intentional disconnection is something that I take into my daily Ceremony, healings, and prayers.

Last Fall, I stood on the very Land near my Father's home territory—*Genaabaajing* (Serpent River)—that holds this deep grief around residential school history, and beneath my feet, it was heavy with stories left untold. I could hear the suppressed voices and the restless spirits of the Land. I could feel the Earth energetically echoing all that still needs to be seen and acknowledged with every step. On that day, my father told me stories of young girls jumping off cliffs to their deaths to get away from missionaries who were coming to sexually assault them. He also spoke of babies born from rape, who were burned in incinerators by the nuns to hide the evidence. In that moment, I realized how unraveling from colonization is a forever journey. When your Spirit, body, and mind are colonized at the hands of the oppressor, parts of you are frozen there. Unraveling from all of this is like a soul retrieval, thawing aspects of trauma and reclaiming our healed selves, bit by bit. As we do this, I believe the Land heals, too. Those are the prayers I placed down upon the Earth that day for myself, my children, my people. That day I also learned of a Grandmother who was a midwife and a Medicine Keeper, for where there is pain, there is healing. Where there is suffering, there is love that needs to be uncovered. The Land whispered the stories. The Spirits informed me of the Medicine, and my heart healed a thousand lifetimes.

"Decolonization" has been a huge buzzword over the past few years. I have noticed that our "journey to decolonize" can become another way to measure each other, another thing to achieve. Shame and guilt may arise, as we might feel like we aren't doing it fast or well enough. But true decolonizing is a forever journey to walk, and if you are currently walking it, it's okay for it to take time. You might never get there fully, but wherever you are on this journey, remember you are enough. If you are like me, it might take you a lifetime to unravel the harm. When we find ourselves moving through colonial energy in our hearts and minds, please remember that your Ancestors were forced into assimilation; it runs deep and is not your fault. A term that better describes the process of unraveling from colonial harm and rooting back into our Medicine ways is "re-Indigenize." This word feels more like a remembering, healing through the trauma to come home and shine a light on what has always been there.

If our Medicines have been stolen, suppressed, or buried, feeling worthy of reclaiming what has been taken can be a barrier to accessing traditional ways. We can work through this by welcoming in compassion for our journey and acknowledging the parts of our Spirit that we ignore. It's essential that we hold ourselves in the light of understanding and tenderness as we do this work. As Porcupine reminded us earlier, release your shame and guilt. Know that this path is calling you for a reason. The Medicine is within you, waiting to rise.

RECLAMATION

Colonization removed me from the spiritual practices that I feel would have best nourished my Indigenous soul. A memory that is deeply ingrained in my mind is when I received my First Communion in the Catholic Church at the age of seven. My Grandparents were so proud, and they gifted me with a rosary. The sentiment was beautiful and in line with what my Grandparents thought being a "good" Catholic meant. The ways of the church were at the forefront of their faith—rooted in their hearts and ways of being. I understand that Spirit can come through different channels, and yet, I wondered why it all seemed to happen within the four walls of a church. The memories that were imprinted were not of my Indigenous Grandparents praying with our Medicines, but rather the religion of the colonizer who stole those teachings away.

Sadly, my story is not unique, and many folks have struggled to reclaim ways that were almost extinguished. I can only speak for my one Indigenous experience and journey of reclamation. It has been a journey of peaks and valleys, doubt and wonder, curiosity and connection. There is not one perfect path to reclaim lost parts of our culture, traditions, and teachings. I dream of an Earth where we can all honor each other's ways of reclamation, as I believe there is not one perfect path. To judge, shame, or belittle another's way of reconnection feeds into the colonial mind-set we are trying to heal from. We might take different paths to reclaim what was lost and stolen. If this is part of your story, I see you and honor you. Part of sharing my Medicine in the way that I do is to invite others to root into their own knowing, to trust the call of their heart and Spirit. If you carry a story of disconnection in your lineage, no matter what the reason is, there is hope. You can reclaim what has been buried. I am a testament to this.

One of the most challenging aspects of my reclaiming has been to learn our original language. It is said that speaking our language is our way of connecting deeply with all our Kin, our Spirit, and the Land. Every day I try to learn a few words and practice them with my children. The fact that our language was stripped away from us is excruciating, and the effects are felt in my generation and those that will follow. I often wonder what might have been different for my path and the path of my descendants if my Ancestors had felt free to share their Medicines in their fullest Anishinaabe expression. I am curious of what could have been different beyond the rosaries, crosses, and Sunday mass. There were moments of language spoken, Ceremony offered, and teachings passed down, but it always seemed to be mixed with the colonial trauma of our past. Like many of us, I can wish for a more straightforward path to reclamation, but sadly it is not my reality. I also reflect on the resilience, courage, and strength it takes to keep our connection to Spirit alive. And for that, I am deeply grateful for all that has been passed down to me and what I carry forward as Medicine into the present and future.

Medicine Reflection: Are there any parts of your own lineage that feel difficult to reclaim? Do you feel worthy of reclaiming them?

INTERGENERATIONAL TRAUMA

The study of epigenetics has been brought to the forefront over the last few years. There is more and more evidence that points to the inherited nature of trauma. Researchers have found that the expression of DNA can be impacted by traumatic experiences of the generations that came before.

You may have heard of the study that tied the scent of cherry blossom to trauma. Researchers introduced acetophenone—a chemical that carries the cherry blossom scent—to mice, blowing it into their cages while they, at the same time, zapped the mice's feet with mild electric currents. Soon the mice associated the smell with the pain of the electric shock. They found that when those mice had pups, their offspring and the subsequent generation of offspring showed signs of anxiety and fear around the scent. The next generations did not have the same response but rather a heightened sensitivity to the scent.

The possibility that memories, painful experiences, suffering, and trauma can be passed down through our DNA is revolutionary. As an Indigenous Person, I can personally attest to the impact of generational trauma on my body and Spirit. Some may say it's anecdotal, yet the most profound inner work of my life has been unraveling layers of Ancestral trauma in my system. I have witnessed it in many of my clients and also in my children. When we hold the possibility that the trauma of our Ancestors is stored in our blood, bones, and Water memory, we are able also to find ways to heal and release this from our bodies and spirits. This allows for a vision and path of ease, joy, wellness, and abundance for the generations to come.

When I was four, I went to my first week of kindergarten. I remember the ache in my belly every day as my mom put me on the bus and said good-bye. Every day, there were tears as I pleaded to not go. The culture of school was too harsh for my sensitive soul, so I spent that year in the safety of home.

When my first son went to kindergarten, he hated it. It was a traumatic year for all of us. There was a day that sent chills down my spine. His teachers were walking him to his classroom, and he said, "Mommy, don't let them take me away." I took him home that day. His lineage is filled with both residential school trauma from my side of the family and Holocaust trauma from his Jewish father's side. I could see the fear of "being taken away" in his eyes. That day is imprinted in my heart forever, and it was that day that I vowed I would heal as much trauma as I possibly could in my system so that my children didn't have to. It showed me why I had such a hard time going into a colonial institution at the age of four. My cells remembered, my son remembered, and I have no doubt in my mind that trauma is inherited, each generation expressing it in their own way.

If we carry intergenerational trauma (and we do),
then we also carry intergenerational wisdom.
It's in our genes and in our DNA.

— KAZU HAGA

LONGING FOR CONNECTION

During my journey of reclamation, I began to share stories of how I was connecting to my Medicine roots by learning from Elders and teachers and engaging in the deep healing of my body, mind, and Spirit. I noticed that many non-Indigenous people could relate. They held space for the stories I shared around the pain that residential schools, oppression, and attempted genocide caused. Due to the nature of this trauma, BIPOC folks and communities from marginalized identities could relate deeply. Many had experienced this pain in their own way and felt the calling to heal through the layers so they could reclaim their Medicine.

As I continued to share, I noticed that this was a story carried by more people than I had initially anticipated, including:

- People who have immigrated or have lost connection to their Land for a variety of reasons.

- People whose Ancestors practiced healing arts and were condemned.

- People who had challenging relationships with their families or felt angry at the Ancestors and wanted nothing to do with them.

- Adoptees with no connection to the Ancestors and culture of their birth families.

The list goes on and on.

The disconnection is real. One of the primary wounds we seem to hold as human beings is that we don't belong. We all have a deep longing to be in relationship with our roots. For many, there is grief around all that has been lost, but there is so much wisdom to find when we start on this healing journey. While it's important to acknowledge the trauma so we can let it rise to be seen and healed, it's vital that we also recognize the wisdom we carry in our DNA. Claiming these Medicine aspects of ourselves and sharing them with the world is part of our rising. It excites me when I witness others digging deep to see the beauty, the power, and the illumination that their lineage holds. Porcupine reminds us that even through the trauma, our wisdom shines bright.

WORTHINESS

Feeling worthy of claiming our stories, teachings, and wisdom can be one of the most challenging parts of reclamation. When our Ancestors have been shamed, we carry shame. When our Ancestors have been disconnected from their Spirit, heart, wisdom, or knowing, we carry this disconnect, too. It is no wonder that it takes some of us a long time to feel worthy of retrieving what was lost, and we must honor ourselves deeply through this journey. It can take a lot to move love through barriers of abuse, shame, denial, and forced assimilation. The truth is that it is a much easier path to learn about different traditional ways when you don't have trauma associated with them. Trauma becomes a barrier to your reclamation. To feel worthy of reclaiming the Medicines of our lineage means that we are willing to look beyond the messages that we have received our entire lives and stand in our power. We must do it for our Ancestors, our descendants, and the Earth. We are worthy because we exist. We are enough because we *are*. Unraveling ourselves from cultural conditioning and trauma through energy work, therapy, community support, and other modalities will help us stand in our worthiness so we can walk in confidence and empowerment. Raspberry Moon invites us into this space: all we need to do is to listen.

FIRST CONTACT

When I was young, my Ancestors would show up in my room as beings, standing beside me or at the foot of my bed. I would be so startled that I would jump up and immediately turn on the light. They would speak different languages to me or sing me songs. At the time, I had no idea what was happening; I was frightened. My sleep and dream time have always been filled with these connections. My seer Medicine would come out at night, and I would travel to my Relations through dreams and journeys, or they would come and visit me in my bedroom as Spirits.

It wasn't until I got older and started to see different Healers that I finally understood what was happening. My Ancestors had been calling to me from a very young age, and when I reached my 20s, I finally could listen. I realized that they were calling to me to activate my path as a Healer and Visionary. They were calling me back home. Since I accepted their invitation and began my reclamation journey, my intentional connection to my Ancestors has been life-giving, and I have built a daily practice of relationship with them.

OF THE STARS

Anishinaabe people call ourselves the Star People. Our origin story speaks of Sky Woman falling through a portal in the Sky from the Stars and bringing the Medicine of life and beauty to the Earth. If you remember our story about Turtle Island, the story of Sky Woman is often part of this Creation legend. Sky Woman spins down from the cosmos and lands on the Turtle shell. With her dance of gratitude and the alchemy of all of her kin, life is activated upon the shell of the Turtle. A beautiful telling of this story can be found in *Braiding Sweetgrass* by Robin Wall Kimmerer. This is why we often say that we are "of the Stars," for this is where we come from. We are made of the same ingredients, essence, and energy. I feel that in our reclamation and remembering, we are trying to understand and come back to this origin of who we are. When we die, this is where we return, the Stars welcoming us home once again.

You may have heard some spiritual people speak about Star Beings or Starseeds, so I think that our origin story speaks to many. In the moments when I have felt the heaviness of this Earth, as a highly sensitive soul, I have heard myself say, "I want to go home"—and I mean the Stars. When I have been in a lupus flare, I feel this pull. It will tug at us in our need and desire to belong. When feelings of not belonging arise with our Earth Kin, we may feel the comfort of those Stars calling us in familiar ways. We are blessed to have our Ancestors shining down upon us, reminding us that we are never alone. They provide us with a gateway to the Star Nations, flooding us with memories of our home.

I've worked with thousands of people from all backgrounds and lineages, and their Ancestors have shown themselves to me in two ways:

1. *Known Ancestors*

   These are Ancestors or family members that you know in the physical realm. They also could be Ancestors that you've heard stories of or those who meant something to your relatives. There is an earthly connection to them in some way.

2. *Star Ancestors*

   These are a realm of Spirit beings who surround us to bring the energy of profound wisdom, support, warmth, and guidance. Star Spirit beings offer unconditional love, truth, and grace.

You may have a different understanding or ways of defining Ancestors, and it's all welcomed here. What is most important is that you nurture your relationship with them.

DISCERNMENT

When we long to be in relationship with our Ancestors, we often begin by calling all of them in, without discernment of who we are inviting into our space. It's such an exciting feeling to open up to new Spirit support, so it's easy to understand why we do this. I did it, too, in my early years of connection, as I wanted to know all of them. While this was helpful to get familiar with their many distinctive energies, I found that as I worked with them more, it was more potent for me to call upon my *healed and well* Ancestors for my spiritual work. It protected me from taking on more responsibility or calling up heaps of trauma, which is especially important if you have a long history of suffering in your lineage. When I use these words or intentions, I have found that even my Ancestors go through their healing cycles. Sometimes the ones I'm used to working with step back, and others come forward. I offer this to you as an invitation to use these words and see what comes forward for you.

MEDICINE JOURNEY
Ancestral Retrieval

Find a comfortable place to sit or lie down, and breathe deeply into your heart. Set an intention to call your Ancestors forward. Is there a name that you used for your relatives? If so, use this now, speak from your heart, and ask them to be present in this space. If not, offer a simple invocation: *I welcome in my healed and well Ancestors.*

Porcupine joins us for this journey, and you see their quills sparkling with light. They lead you onto a path where you find yourself standing on the Lands of your Ancestors. Feel the bottoms of your feet warming with that connection with the Land and your heart warming with the presence of your Ancestors.

Porcupine offers you a golden quill and you hold this up to the Sky to make an intention to call down a healed Ancestor. The quill vibrates, and your hands are instantly lit up with Starlight. You welcome your Ancestor's presence down into your energy field.

Welcome them before you and ask:

Who are you?

What Medicine do you bring?

What are you here to remind me of that I have forgotten?

This Ancestor holds your hands in theirs, and you feel this incredible energy radiating through your mind, body, and Spirit. This Ancestor then asks you:

What can I help you with? What's an intention that I can hold for you today?

You share with them, and they take the answer into their Spirit. They promise to wrap your prayer with the Medicine of the thousands that came before you. They soar back up into the Stars, and you feel a sense of love and protection. *You are the Medicine.* Gently breathe yourself back to your seat and space, and when you feel ready, you can slowly open your eyes.

Medicine Reflection: What are the messages your Ancestor gifted to you?

Ancestral Honoring

When you connect to an Ancestor in a new way, it's always good practice to continue to honor the relationship daily. In my late teens and early 20s, I would move through cycles of body pain that would keep me in bed. My mother and I would pray to our Ancestors for help and healing, and she taught me to put a plate of food out for them because they would get hungry after helping. Feasting with our Ancestors is a beautiful practice passed down to me, and when we offer traditional foods to them, it makes the practice very meaningful, although any food is a blessing.

Some other ideas for building and nurturing this connection:

- Place pictures of your Ancestors on your altar or Medicine Bundle.

- Put an offering other than food down upon the Earth (Plant Medicine, a strand of your hair, a stone or crystal, a song) when you want to offer gratitude to them.

- Practice calling them in when you are connecting, praying, or facilitating healing for others.

- Sit with your Elders and ask them to tell you stories about your lineage.

ANCESTRAL REMEMBERING

Even though my Ancestors showed up in Spirit most nights of my youth, I remained disconnected from their messages and their wisdom. They remained persistent in their call, and finally, one day, my receptivity cracked open. When I was diagnosed with lupus, I found out that pharmaceuticals and the medical system were not the only things that were going to help me. Buried deep under the harm of colonization were the ways of those who came before me. I was guided to the Earth, Spirit connection, and healing in ways beyond what my naked eye could see. Lupus was a gift that led me back to my most authentic self. It helped me remember that the Medicine I needed was within me, waiting to be unearthed from my dreams, visions, blood, and bones. I began to remember.

Remembering has come to me in different ways. Due to the trauma and disconnect, our ways have not always been passed down with ease. Sometimes we don't have direct access to our Elders, our lineage, or our village. Sadly, we don't live in a community the way we used to. How do we gain the wisdom we crave or receive the richness of the Medicines of our lineage? Some folks are blessed to have spent their entire lives with their Elders, Guides, and family members, who pass down their traditions, Medicine ways, and teachings. It lights up my heart when I hear these stories, and if this is your experience, continue to honor the ways that this has been passed down to you and continue to move it into future generations. You are needed.

If this wasn't your experience, I believe that there are many other ways to gain knowing respectfully. A Medicine Woman once told me that there was a Grandmother Spirit who visited me in my dreams when I was a little girl. She would braid my hair and infuse each strand of hair with our teachings and Medicine Ways. When she shared this with me, tears streamed down my face. I had always wondered why I "knew" certain things yet didn't remember anyone intentionally teaching me these things.

As I grew, these ways would come forward through dreams, visions, and journeys. As I paid more attention, deeper learning continued through all of my healing work with energy Healers, Shamans, Visionaries, and therapists. Bit by bit, it felt like I was unearthing the knowing that was waiting for me to bring it into my awareness and consciousness. This knowing would get rooted as wisdom. Over the years, I have gratefully received Ancestral teachings through Elders, Guides, and others. The most potent teachings have come through my own experience, whether during a healing session, in Dreamtime, or in a vision. We all have different ways of reclaiming and restoring harmony to the harm of the past. Your way is needed.

Here are some ways to access wisdom:

1. *Honor the space of your Dreamtime.*

   Ask your Ancestors to offer you teachings at night or help you to journey to retrieve them.

2. *Build a relationship with the Plant, Tree, and Flower People.*

   Speak to them, grow them, listen to them, hug them, love them. These beings will communicate beautiful and wise Medicine to your heart and Spirit.

3. *Take Medicine journeys.*

   The journeys in this book are attuned to assist you in retrieving your inner knowing and wisdom. As you listen or read through the book, we are building pathways of remembering together. Trust.

4. *Pay attention to your body.*

   Your body always knows. Trust the tears that spring to your eyes or the warmth in your heart when you feel deep resonance with something you hear, read, or engage with, for they are powerful signs.

5. *Ask your Ancestors to guide you to the right teachers.*

   The right Guides will help you activate, remember, and heal through any blocks to your reclamation.

6. *Be open to the magic of synchronicity in your life.*

As Wayne Dyer said, "I am realistic—I expect miracles." There is Wisdom all around you and within, waiting to be integrated and birthed through you. Open your eyes and your heart to all of Creation waiting to serve and support your growth.

RESPONSIBILITY AND BOUNDARIES

In order to be born, you needed: 2 parents, 4 grandparents, 8 great-grandparents, 16 second great-grandparents, 32 third great-grandparents, 64 fourth great-grandparents, 128 fifth great-grandparents, 256 sixth great-grandparents, 512 seventh great-grandparents, 1,024 eighth great-grandparents, 2,048 ninth great-grandparents. For you to be born today from the 12 previous generations, you needed a total of 4,094 Ancestors over the last 400 years.

— LYRICAL ZEN

"You are the chosen one, Asha, here to heal much of your Ancestors' pain," he said.

I was in my late 20s at the time, studying shamanism and doing lots of my own shadow healing work. I felt my Ancestors standing around me, and I told them that I would rise to the challenge and take on this responsibility and carry the burden. Over the years, I continued to hear similar messages during healing sessions, and I continued to dive deep into healing the wounds and struggles of my Ancestors. After years of doing this and straining myself physically and emotionally, I finally realized that I couldn't do it anymore.

Robyn Moreno—a Curandera and friend—reminded me one day that my Ancestors walked and healed through so much so that I didn't have to. That reframing was so powerful for me. All 4,094 Ancestors did not have to process their trauma through my body. I could be free, light, and well.

I had agreed to carry too heavy of a burden, and I knew that I was not meant to constantly struggle under this weight. I was meant to thrive. I did some significant healing work around shifting contracts and agreements and set a boundary with my Ancestors. Every day when I would call them in, I envisioned a fire around my body that would help transmute and clear their pain. I prayed to them and told them that I was now setting this boundary. After a few months of doing this, I saw that it was to my Ancestors' benefit for me to be well and that they wanted this for me, too. As I did my healing work, I promised that I would offer them the transformative love that flowed from me. I stood for my energy, body, and system, knowing that I matter, too. I affirmed my vision of wellness for my children and the seven generations to come. It was a heavy load to shake off my shoulders, but those boundaries were necessary for me to rise in my Medicine and thrive. If you feel that burden, perhaps it might speak to you to set some boundaries with your Ancestors, too. Like Porcupine says, you deserve to be free of guilt and shame. You are worthy of wellness.

TEACHINGS FROM THE SPIRIT WORLD

Recently, my paternal Grandmother passed away. One afternoon while I was meditating, I felt her Spirit leave this realm and pass into another. I had these unique body sensations and a feeling of lightness. The same thing happened when my maternal Grandfather passed away. It was like layers of trauma that I was carrying from being their descendant were now instantly lifted from my body, mind, and Spirit. I put some Tobacco down in gratitude for this, as I know that in their Earthly form, they couldn't help me with this healing; but now in their Spirit form, they could take what I didn't need to carry.

Due to the trauma that they carried around upon this Earth, my grandparents weren't able to pass down the language, Ceremonies, or Medicines that I was trying to reclaim, and that's okay. It has become clear that their communication with me from the Spirit World is potent and profound. Recently, my clairaudience abilities have gotten stronger. Usually, I perceive messages from Spirit through visions or knowing, but now I can hear clearly. I believe this is a gift my recently passed Grandmother has offered to me. Her journey to the Spirit World cleared something so that I could embody my gifts more deeply. My Grandfather shows up every morning with visions, direction, and guidance for me while I shower. The Water is a beautiful transmitter of sacred information. I am so grateful that they can now offer me guidance from a healed place and trauma no longer blocks my access to our Medicine Ways.

Walking. I am listening in a deeper way. Suddenly, all my Ancestors are behind me. Be still, they say. Watch and listen. You are the result of the love of thousands.

— LINDA HOGAN, NATIVE AMERICAN WRITER

Porcupine Medicine Invocation

Dearest Porcupine, I invite you to help me release the guilt, shame, and trauma that prevent me from fully accessing the Medicines, Ceremonies, rituals, and teachings of my Ancestors. Help me to turn harshness into healing. When I feel all alone, remind me that I have the protection of thousands of Ancestral beings all around me. I am grateful for your presence in my life because you remind me that I came here to shine a light on what needs to be healed in the past—to be who I am in the present.

Mskomini Giizis Moon Affirmation

I allow this Moon of reclamation to amplify my connection with my well and vital Ancestors. May I continue to feel worthy of reclaiming the Medicine that lives in my bones and blood. I am the Medicine.

CHAPTER 9

DATKAAGMIIN GIIZIS BLACKBERRY MOON

Our eighth Moon of Creation shares the gift of the Blackberry with us, which is said to be one of the original plants placed on the Earth. This extra Moon only happens every few years, usually in July or August. It asks us to listen carefully, to pay attention to what is trying to awaken our Spirit so that we may walk the right path of our life. This Moon encourages our connection to the Spirit World, reminding us that our Guides are waiting to show us the way—success is waiting, and we have the ability to attract a beautiful unfolding.

MOON LEGEND: HOW BLACKBERRY LED THE WAY

Blackberry was created in the early days, where there was a lot of darkness and quiet. They had a lot of time to listen to their heart, to pay attention, and to reflect. As the Earth began to fill with other Plants and Animals, Blackberry would watch the diverse and beautiful energies come to life. They watched Otter learn to swim, Dandelion's seeds blow in the wind, and Rainbow come after the storm. They were quieter than other aspects of Creation, as they had learned to listen more than they spoke. They had lived for many Moons and became the wise one that the Plants and Animals would come to when they needed guidance.

Every time a being had a question, Blackberry would lead the questioner back to themselves and ask them: "What does your Spirit say?" "How does your Heart feel?" "What are your dreams telling you?" "How is the Land informing you?" Some of the Animals and Plants would feel frustrated. All they wanted was for Blackberry to tell them the answers! Sometimes they even begged Blackberry to tell them what to do. But Blackberry stayed rooted in their knowing, trusting that all would reveal itself in time, with reflection and deep listening.

With Blackberry modeling how to receive inner wisdom, all of Creation began to practice this way of being, going within for their answers, listening to the guidance of the Earth, and building their intuition and knowing. Every day they would close their eyes and invite the Spirit World to inform their knowing. It was a powerful approach to living and each aspect of Creation became a sovereign being. Because there was less self-doubt, fighting, competition, and comparison ceased to exist. The world had become a beautiful place because of Blackberry, and one day the Plants came to ask if they could make Blackberry the Chief of the Land.

As they approached Blackberry with this request, they were met with a gentle and humble smile. "Dearest Kin, you are all powerful in your own right. I stand beside you, not above you. If you would like to give back, all I ask is that you continue to trust in your connection to the Spirit World. Your Medicine wisdom is waiting to be awakened. Stand tall in the gifts Creator has given you and find your way of leading in this world. We all have a way—my job was to simply remind you of that." And from that day forward, all of Creation walked beside one another, acknowledging the gifts they carried and valuing the beauty of one another.

Animal Spirit: *Ajijaak* (Crane)

The Animal Spirit that best represents our eighth Moon of Creation is Crane, or as they are known in Anishiinabemowin, *Ajijaak*. This animal is a masterful communicator and helps to guide our connection with our inner self and the Spirit realm. Crane reminds us that we all have a story to tell and wisdom to impart. As we walk carefully with integrity and balance, we can mentor and serve others with the inherent knowing we carry. Sometimes the most information comes to us in stillness and quiet, and Crane asks us to listen carefully to draw from all that is being offered to steer us in the right direction and awaken the Medicine within.

Crane Message

- There is great power in observation.
- Protect your peace.
- Awaken the gifts within.
- Prosperity and luck are on your side.

THE CLAN SYSTEM

As an Anishiinaabe Woman of the Ojibwe nation, my kinship system is based on a Clan or Totem. In Anishiinabemowin, the word for this is *Dodem*, which, if you say aloud, sounds like the word "Totem." Our Clan system continues to be an important part of our identity. It helps us identify what responsibilities each Clan has in building and maintaining community. Some are here to mediate, plan, and negotiate; others are here to heal, nourish, and offer Medicines. Some Clans are more connected to the teachings of the Waters and the Stars, while others are the protectors and warriors. We believe that Creator gifted us this system to maintain balance in our communities.

The Clan System supports my deep knowing and message that we each are here for a particular purpose, and the more we claim our role on this Earth, the more we rise in our Medicine. We cannot be and do all things. Imagine a world where each of us fully honored what was dreamed and envisioned for us by our Creator? Imagine we followed that path, never doubting that clear message of knowing from within. There would be less jealousy and envy of another's path. There would be less comparison and judgment of what others are doing. We would all stand tall in our own sacred resonance and work together, supporting each other in our rise. This honoring of our purpose and that of another is my dream and vision. And I see it rooted in the Clan System.

Ojibwe Clans

- **Turtle Clan (*Mikinaak Dodem*)** – Healers, Teachers, Wellness, Cleansing

- **Crane Clan *(Ajijaak Dodem)*** – Leadership, Speaking, Gifted with Oral Tradition

- **Deer Clan *(Waawaashkeshi Dodem)*** – Agility, Graciousness, Kindness

- **Bear Clan *(Mkwa Dodem)*** – Protection, Strength, Traditional Plant Knowledge

- **Porcupine Clan** *(Gaag Dodem)* – Warriors, Land Defenders, Protectors

- **Sturgeon Clan** *(Name Dodem)* – Wisdom Keepers, Ancestral Connection, Royal Esteem

- **Butterfly Clan** *(Memengwaa Dodem)* – Beauty, Healers, Wellness, Transformation

- **Eagle Clan** *(Migizi Dodem)* – Visionaries, Freedom, Creativity

- **Thunderbird Clan** *(Binasi Dodem)* – Protection, Healer, Guardianship

- **Loon Clan** *(Maang Dodem)* – Peacemakers, Beauty, Singing from the Heart

- **Wolf Clan** *(Ma'iingan Dodem)* – Guardianship, Community, Responsibility

- **Marten Clan** *(Waabizheshi Dodem)* – Hunters, Gatherers, Creators

  (These teachings were adapted from *Ojibway Clans: Animal Totems and Spirits* by Mark Anthony Jacobson)

As you can see, everyone plays a particular role, honoring their greatest gifts and natural tendencies. Your individual nature is valuable and essential to the harmony of the community as a whole. We celebrate everyone's unique talents, and ours are honored and respected too. We work together in a reciprocal way to create beauty and harmony. This sounds like a brilliant world to me; may we remember these teachings, always.

Because my lineage holds the Medicines of different Anishinaabe Ancestors, it has been shared that we are part of the Crane, Bear, Deer, and Thunderbird Clans. I have chosen to claim the clan passed down matrilineally through my Grandfather. As a member of the Crane Clan *(Ajijaak Dodem)*, I often reflect on what type of leader I want to be. Leadership holds great responsibility. I believe we can lead with grace and wisdom, and I intend to unravel old colonial energies that tell us we must lead with authority. Abusing our power as leaders is something to be mindful of every day. I take the responsibility to create brave spaces, lead with love and vision, and honor all who sit in circle with me.

Crane Clan people are the speakers, important in continuing our oral tradition. I love being invited to speak and share through my voice and energy. I also love offering my Medicine through guided journeys and healing activations and feel that this is one of the best ways my gifts are expressed. My Clan is here to encourage and uplift others, and it is my favorite thing to shine a light on the Medicines others hold and help them spread their wings to fly.

Medicine Reflection: What Clan do you resonate with the most?

THE ART OF ASKING QUESTIONS

As a homeopath, I got to ask my patients a lot of questions—and I did a lot of listening. I learned how to track subtle expressions and energies and tune in to what the person may not be saying but wanted to express in other ways. I learned really quickly that our answers are usually buried underneath our stories. The patient always had wisdom within waiting to come forward, they just needed the right question to help them uncover it.

As my practice turned into more of an energetic healing practice, I would use what I had learned in homeopathy and apply it to my healing sessions. We would journey and the client would see, sense, or feel certain truths. When I held space for that to be uncovered, deep healing occurred. I saw that it was actually more powerful for the client to discover the truth or vision than for me to tell them what I saw. Yes, I could see their Ancestors and Guides around them. I could see what Past Lives or messages the Spirit World were offering, yet sharing what I saw didn't land as deeply as when their own guidance came forward. I learned to step back and get my ego out of the way. I am not an authority over anyone. I believe the best Healer is one who leads and guides you back to yourself. Like Crane reminds us, you are a sovereign, powerful, and wise being; you can lead yourself. If anyone tries to make you feel otherwise, please walk away.

> **Medicine Reflection:** Do you trust your inner knowing? How often do you look for answers outside yourself? What has your experience been?

ANIMAL SPIRIT AWAKENING

It was early in my homeopathic practice days, and I had my clipboard on my lap and was taking case notes. The woman who sat before me was experiencing anxiety and depression. She expressed that she felt lost and directionless. She hated her job and felt like she needed a change but couldn't find the energy to make the change. As I listened to her speak, I saw a Horse galloping around her. It felt so real, like a wind passing by my head, my hair lifting as it ran by. I remember wondering why the heck I was seeing an Animal. It wasn't my usual practice to share what I was seeing around my clients, but this Horse was very persistent. I nervously shared it with her and her face lit up. She told me that she loved horseback riding as a child and it brought her so much joy. I asked her to close her eyes and imagine her favorite horse standing before her. Her whole body shifted before my eyes. Tears ran down her face, and she told me that she couldn't believe she had forgotten these parts of herself. I ended up prescribing a remedy for the anxiety and depression, which I do believe supported her; but to this day, I believe that Horse Spirit was a huge part of her finding her joy again. I asked her to connect to this Horse daily when she took her remedy, and when she came for a follow up, she told me she was feeling alive and inspired to find a new path.

Animals kept showing up in these ways in my practice, along with Ancestors, Angelic Beings, and other Guides. I knew that they were an important part of what I was meant to incorporate in my healing work. I began to see that the Animals that came forward were forgotten aspects of my clients—Medicine gifts that they held and had somehow been disconnected from. Every time they did a guided meditation or journey with me to find an Animal, they brought aspects of themselves forward from their subconscious. I would see the light in their eyes and the awakening in their hearts as they remembered. It has been such a sacred and beautiful part of my path of service.

> **Medicine Reflection:** Have you ever connected to an Animal Spirit? In what ways did they help you remember who you are?

WORKING WITH THE ANIMAL REALM

Although I have already mentioned this in a few places throughout this book, it bears repeating when we speak of working with Animal Spirits/Totems/Medicine. We must always honor these beings as sacred and come from a place of reciprocity. Colonial thinking has conditioned us to take and extract. We must remember that our connection to this realm is a gift, not a commodity.

Although Animal Spirit Medicine is not solely based in North American Indigenous practices, it is vital to honor the lineages and the lived experience of those who have carried these teachings in their lives since time immemorial. Do the work to see those who are marginalized and invisible. While it might not seem relevant to the discussion of Animal Spirits, it is all related. Show up with humility and reciprocity, and you will walk in a good way.

Animal Spirits can appear from the Spirit realm, in your dreams, visions, or journeys, or they can appear in a very earthly way; for example, you have a bird fly across your windshield, or a family of raccoons take up space in your attic. They can also appear in synchronistic ways; for example, your child asks for a particular stuffed animal, and then you see the animal on television and in a magazine. Just like the Blackberry Moon teaches us to listen deeply to the subtle signs all around us, stay curious and open to where Spirit Animals want to show up and let the Medicine bless you. The Animal domain encompasses all living creatures, including birds, insects, reptiles, et cetera, and there is no hierarchy of one being better than another.

Medicine Reflection: Have you ever felt drawn to an Animal without being able to explain why? Have you felt fear around a particular Animal? What do you sense these Animals were trying to tell you?

Creation Story Animal

In my experience, we each have one Animal we are connected to from the time we are arrive here in this life. They show up as allies in our Mother's womb space and carry a Medicine that is connected to our biggest life lesson. They will appear when something we thought we had healed rises up again for us to take a deeper look. For example, Deer walks with me as a reminder that I frequently need to soften. Deer is here to help me release shame and deepen into self-love. As I move through the ebbs and flows of my evolution as a person, this Animal will weave in and out of my life.

Medicine Reflection: Take a moment to close your eyes and place your hand over your heart. Call forward on your inner wise one and ask them: "What Animal came with me for my biggest life lesson and why?" Trust what you receive.

Ally Animal

As we walk our path, other Animals may show up as allies or helpers that guard and protect our space and inform our steps. These Animals are ones that are present to be called upon when needed, and if you develop a relationship with them, hang out in your energy field. The allies that journey with me daily are Bear and Eagle: Bear helps me to set the boundaries that I need and offers rest as Medicine, and Eagle helps me stay true to my vision.

Medicine Reflection: Are there any Animals that you feel protect or guard you?

Blessing Animal

Last, on our beautiful journey of life, there are different Animals who will join us at different times on our path. Maybe it's an Animal you see when you're walking in the forest, or perhaps you dream about one. Maybe it's on a card that you pull from an oracle card deck or appears when someone else is doing a reading. These Animals are asking you to build a relationship with them for the time being, but they may flow out of your life when their Medicine and magic are complete. A decade ago, my aunt died from lupus, and before she died, she told me that she would come back as a Bear. The evening of her funeral, a Bear ran across the road in front of my mother. As I was writing this chapter, a beautiful Blue Heron landed five feet away from me. Blue Herons are always a sign that my Grandfather is near. You might find that you, too, have an animal that represents someone who has passed on to the other side. I believe that they can visit us through these sightings, reminding us that we are never alone and they are never truly gone.

> **Medicine Reflection:** Is there an Animal that reminds you of someone close to you who has passed on? Is there a particular sensation or sign that it's a visitor from the Spirit World?

HONORING YOUR CONNECTION

As with any other relationship, our Animal Spirit connections deserve intentional care. Here are some suggestions of how to nourish and nurture your relationship:

- Gifting them with a song, prayer, or plant offering.

- Offering words of invocation as you step into ritual or Ceremony with them.

- Repeating gratitude prayers when you wake and before bed.

- Placing an image of them on your altar or space where you pray.

- Watching for their presence, knowing that with every meeting, your connection strengthens.

MEDICINE JOURNEY
Find Your Animal Spirit

Find a comfortable place to sit or lie down, and breathe deeply. Sink deeply into your surroundings. As you breathe, I invite you to release all expectations of what Animal may come forward. Open your heart, open your Spirit, and allow yourself to receive. A golden door appears before you; it radiates with rainbow light. You are drawn toward it and through it. Feel your feet upon a grounded path; you feel held by sturdy ground. As you look up, you see Blackberry Moon in the Sky; it's early morning and the Moon is still bright. It calls you to remember your connection to the Spirit World and your innate knowing.

As you continue to walk, the Sun begins to rise, and you see Crane standing at the edge of an ancient forest before you. It is filled with tall, majestic Trees with inviting branches, and Crane welcomes you in. They remain at the edge of the forest, guarding the space. As you enter you experience the scents of the beautiful Plants and Trees that surround you. The Medicines fill up your lungs, opening your heart center, readying you to receive the guidance you are searching for. You walk deeper and deeper into the forest and notice a clearing in the distance. You begin to hear rustling and feel a vibrant wind blow by your face. The energy in the forest comes alive, radiant with Spirit. A bright beam of light shines down before you; it's so illuminated that you instantly take a deep breath. Appearing before you in this light is an Animal. Trust what you see. They get clearer in their appearance, and you see their eyes glowing with golden light. Breathe again deeply and invite them into your space.

You ask them three questions:

What are the Medicines that you are bringing to me today?

You listen with your ears, your heart, and your Spirit, and they answer you.

What have I forgotten about myself that you are here to remind me of?

You listen with your ears, your heart, and your Spirit, and they answer you.

What is the next best healing step that I can take toward my wholeness?

You listen with your ears, your heart, and your Spirit, and they answer you.

This Animal wishes to offer you a brilliant activation so that you can embody their Medicine more fully. They transmute into a sparkling, luminescent vibration and ask if you want to receive this healing. As you walk forward to meld with their energy, you feel the warmth and unconditional love move through your body, mind, and Spirit. Breathe deeply as you receive this from the top of your head to the soles of your feet. You become the Animal. *You are the Medicine.*

You move out of this forest space, passing Crane and thanking them for holding space. The Animal Medicine you connected to continues to flow through you. You notice you are moving differently. Feel the vibration and blessing of this Animal pulsing through you with every step you take. It's a powerful sensation, and you take as much time as you need. You honor this experience by offering this Animal a gift. Nurture the relationship in your own way. This Animal will be with you until you no longer need their Medicine.

As you walk through the door, you feel yourself coming back to your own body, rooted, grounded, and illuminated with this beauty. You breathe and slowly open your eyes.

> **Medicine Reflection:** What Animal came forward for you today? What aspects of yourself have you forgotten that you are now encouraged to claim?

ANIMAL GIFTS AND WISDOM

Over the years, the Animal realm has gifted me with energy practices that I can use for myself and those I work with. When I laid my hands down, they would channel their Medicine through me to gift extra protection, guidance, and love. Here are a few of the practices that I use often. You may even find your own version with different Animal Medicines.

Whenever we use these practices, we start with gratitude and respect and ask for permission. Your invocation may look something like this: *Dearest Animal Spirit, may I receive the gift you have to offer me? I reach out to you with gratitude and honoring and vow to continue building a sacred relationship with you.*

1. *Bear Medicine Fur*

    Call upon Bear Medicine. Envision a fur coat that is offered to your energy field. Zip it up to cover yourself from head to toe. Useful for when your vitality feels depleted. Also suitable

for boundary setting when you need to say
no or have not honored your boundaries.
This fur coat will soothe your nervous system
into safety.

2. *Turtle Medicine Shell*

Call upon Turtle Medicine. Envision a Turtle
shell beneath your feet. Gently move your feet
upon it to activate it. Feel the stability it offers
you, balancing you and rooting you down.
Useful for when you feel scattered, ungrounded,
or as though you have "left" your body. Helpful
when you find yourself feeling fearful. This
will help to remind you that it's safe to be here,
present in your physical body.

3. *Wolf Medicine Growl*

Call upon Wolf Medicine. Envision it walking
around you, circling your energy field. Ask for
its fierce protection to come forward; envision
it baring its teeth and growling. Useful for
when you feel like you need extra protection
from jealousy, envy, projection, or wounding
being sent your way. This growl will help you to
maintain your energy, vital force, and peace.

4. *Butterfly Medicine Wings*

Call upon Butterfly Medicine. Place your
hands over your heart, and feel the warmth of
love fill you up and move into your shoulder
blades—feel the gentle flutter of your wings
birthing from your back, extending out and
growing. Stand tall, heart open, Spirit shining

in transformation. Useful for when you have moved through a death and rebirth, from shadow to light. This wing expansion will help to align you into the next stage of your evolution.

5. *Raven Shapeshift*

Envision a Raven before you. Their wings spread out wide and cast a shadow in front of you. You step into this shadow and immerse yourself in their vast, magical Medicine. Feel yourself aligning with empowerment and presence. Feel the magnificence of the wings you hold. This energy acts as a cape to hide you when you need protection or boundaries to be unseen or invisible. Useful for when you feel extra vulnerable or "seen" and you feel the need to shapeshift into another form so that you can stay balanced.

DREAMTIME ANIMALS

The one way that Animals show up consistently for me is in my dreams. I dream of Orcas often, and I have come to know that they show up to remind me that my Medicine is helping others find their soul song. I dreamed of a Moose licking my face and kissing me, which was during a time that I was afraid of dying. Moose came to bring longevity Medicine. Eagle and Hawk feathers show up a lot in my dreams, too, reminding me to stay true to my vision despite what outside voices may be saying. My mother dreams of Snakes, an Animal that she fears during the day yet brings deep Medicine at night. I treat my Dreamtime as deeply sacred, making sleep a priority for my wellness. I have a dream altar beside my bed with my favorite Plant Medicines and crystals, and I clear my bedroom with Smoke Medicine often to keep the space purified. Before bed I will ask for my channel to be open, inviting the Spirit World to inform me while I'm sleeping. I am so grateful that the Animal Spirits hear me. Blackberry Moon reminds us that we are always connected to the Spirit World—sometimes we just need practice making that connection to hear its wisdom and feel its protection.

Medicine Reflection: What is an invocation that you could use to call upon the Animal Spirit realm before bed? Try it out tonight and see what happens.

Crane Medicine Invocation

Dearest Crane, I am ready to rise into who I am meant to be. Help me to remember this when I lose sight of myself. I am ready to build and strengthen my connection with the Spirit World; help me to find more quiet moments in which I can listen to my innate wisdom. Remind me that I carry good Medicine, and it's time to share it with the world. There is nobody quite like me, and I invite you to bring me back to this truth when I forget.

Datkaagmiin Giizis Moon Affirmation

I allow this Moon of spiritual connection to continue to nourish my daily relationship with my support team. May I be curious and listen to the call of the Animals, and may I walk humbly and with gratitude. I am the Medicine.

CHAPTER 10

MDAAMIIN GIIZIS
CORN MOON

Our ninth Moon of Creation shares the teachings of Corn. This Moon happens when Summer is turning to Fall, in September. When we look at a corn cob, we see rows of seeds. It is said that this represents the Spirits of the next generations, the future ones who are being dreamed into being. We must do what we can to prepare for them. Every part of our healing work affects our future descendants, whether they are birthed from us or not. The Spirits of the future are watching and waiting to come and begin their journey on the Earth. During this Moon, we welcome them, and we hold space for their rising through the initiation of our own.

Moon Legend: Why Corn Grew Seeds on Their Body

When Corn was created, they asked if they could be enveloped in a silky husk, for they wanted to slowly acclimatize to their Earth walk because their time in the Stars had felt so miraculous. Creator agreed and planted them on the Earth in a tall stalk so Corn could still feel their connection to the Upper Worlds. The silky husk kept Corn safe and secure, protected from the scorching heat and the downpours of rain. One day, Corn told Creator that they felt ready to explore the Earth plane. They knew they had a purpose and wanted to share it with their Kin.

The hands of Creator reached down and held them; with a burst of love, Creation filled their space. Light began to fill the inside of their husk, and the most beautiful thing happened. Seeds sprouted all over their body; in fact, they spread in beautiful rows all lined up. Each seed carried its own unique Spirit with hopes, dreams, and visions for their futures. Corn was fed by their illuminated souls, and joy filled their heart. They reached up to Grandfather Sun, and all of a sudden, their silky husk broke apart. They radiated in the glory of their fullness, and their seeds were ready to root into their Earth journey.

Corn fed, nourished, and loved all the seeds deeply. Corn taught the seeds what they knew, imparted the wisdom they had, and when it was time to let them go, Corn did just that. The seeds fell to the Earth and lived out their missions. These seeds grew into their own manifestations and fed many of their Kin. The next generations soared in their own way, rising into the beings that Corn had envisioned for them. They learned that they would cultivate much abundance when they collaborated with the Bean and Squash plants. Named one of the "Three Sisters," Corn became a staple in Indigenous diets and continues to grow these rows of seeds to carry out the vision of the generations to come.

Animal Spirit: *Migizi* (Eagle)

The Animal Spirit that best represents our ninth Moon of Creation is the Eagle, or as they are known in Anishiinabemowin, *Migizi*. With their Medicine of vision, a higher perspective, and rising, Eagle is a gateway to our spiritual path; we spread our wings and remember our wholeness when we walk with this Medicine. Traditionally, Eagle carries our prayers and intentions to Creator when we smudge. When gifted, an Eagle feather is an incredible honor in our culture signifying leadership. It indicates that the recipient is rising into their deepest Medicine gifts. With Eagle, we hold our vision of what a healed existence could look like, both for ourselves, our descendants, and the planet.

Eagle Message

- It's time to rise and soar.
- A higher perspective is needed—vision is Medicine.
- Spread your wings to fly.
- Your legacy is waiting.

DESCENDANTS

Although this Moon speaks of the Spirits of the next generation, I know that many have chosen not to have children or cannot have children. Please know that you, too, impact the next generations with your intentions of reclamation, remembrance, and walking in your Medicine. Whether we birth children through our bodies or not, by showing up consciously to heal our past and present, we contribute to a healed vision of the future, on the Land and with each other. Perhaps you see your descendants as aspects of Creation: the Animals, the Plant beings, the Waters. Walking graciously and consciously impacts the whole Circle of Life.

Another way to look at the teachings of the Corn Moon is to think about the legacy that you are leaving behind with your Medicine Walk. How will the steps you take today impact the future? How will they contribute to the well-being of all of your siblings, the Land, the next generations? How will your remembering and rising contribute to raising the consciousness of this planet? How will you lead?

The potential of your impact on this Earth is far-reaching and infinite. This Moon calls us to this great responsibility. We only have this one beautiful life, and during this time, we are being called to live it well.

A Vision for the Future

Ten years ago, I received a vital message twice in that same year. An astrologer told me the baby I was carrying had a soul purpose that was directly connected to mine. I remember the picture that she drew, his soul weaved into mine, as though the wisdom that came from the Stars was directly speaking to him through me. Later that year, I was feeling scared to step into a new version of leadership and I had a psychic reading. This person told me that if I did not step up and shine in the ways that my Ancestors dreamed for me, that my son would not fulfill his life purpose. I heard the echo of the astrologer's words in her message, and it sent chills down my spine. I have never forgotten that moment. Every time I want to shrink or hide, every time I want to quit and give up, every time I doubt my mission here, I look into the beautiful green eyes that my eldest carries, and I remember, this is not only about me. How I choose to show up in the world will directly impact the future and how my children may or may not choose to shine in their own Medicine Walk.

As they have grown, I have noticed the different ways that walking in my Medicine has impacted my children indirectly. They learn through my action, my commitment to our ways—filling our home with traditional teachings and Medicine. One Spring, I started singing and drumming with them. They learned our Water song very quickly. Soon after we were out for a walk, and my son went down to the river on his own and gently started singing to the Water. Tears filled my eyes as he did this without any prompting from me. The Medicine was flowing through him naturally. All the work that I have done and continue to do to unravel the impacts of colonization is moving through to my children. They could share our Medicines freely and beautifully without the shame and guilt previous generations have felt. Corn Moon reminds us to never underestimate the ways your heart, your words, impact this world. For even if you carry the softest and most gentle voice, you are changing the landscape of the generations to come.

Around the time I was gearing up to write the chapter on colonization, the same son announced to my husband and me that he was writing a book. When we inquired what it was going to be about, he told us, "Racism." He spoke compassionately about skin color and ways we can heal. I thought back to those readings 10 years ago and remembered that he would walk in my footsteps. In that moment I was compelled to write about some of the trauma, so one day, he wouldn't have to. I will never know if that will make a difference, but my hope is for my children to walk in wellness and pride in who they are. Part of my Medicine vision is that I inspire my Indigenous children and, on a broader scale, Indigenous youth. I want them to know that they are not invisible, less than, or broken. I want them to know that healing is available to them in their dreams, visions, and quiet moments with the Land. Just like the Corn Moon asks us to vision a healed way for our descendants, I want them to remember their connection to Spirit, their language, their drum songs, and the whispers of their Ancestors. I want to remind them to keep going. Healing is possible. Always.

MEDICINE JOURNEY
Remember Your Legacy

Find a comfortable place to sit or lie down, and pay attention to your breathing. Set an intention to reclaim, remember, and root your legacy down here upon the Earth. We call upon Eagle Medicine to assist us in this journey. Eagle appears before you in some way. They call you to join them on this journey and offer to take you on a ride. You climb onto their back, and they spread their giant wings and take off. You rise higher and higher, soaring through the bright blue Sky and the clouds. The Stars call out to you, "Welcome home, beautiful one," and you soar toward the Cosmos.

The energy around you gets more and more expansive, and you soar to the twinkling Stars. A vortex of energy appears before you, and you jump off Eagle and enter it. As you move through, you begin to see, sense, or know what you came here to do and why.

You ask the supportive energies:

Show me the seeds I am meant to plant as my legacy.

The Star Nations offer you an image, a sensation, a knowing, or words.

Show me the dreams I am meant to nurture.

The Star Nations offer you an image, a sensation, a knowing, or words.

Show me the ripples of impact that I am meant to make in this world.

The Star Nations offer you an image, a sensation, a knowing, or words.

You swirl in the energy in this vortex, which supports you and helps you remember it all clearly. Allow it to move through all of the layers of your being.

As you exit the vortex, Eagle is waiting for you and they offer you wings so that you may soar and leave behind the trail of impact you are here to make.

Feel these wings birthing from the back of your heart and soar back down to Earth. As your feet touch the Land, your wings come back into your heart, and you notice that you are surrounded in Stardust. Gently shake some of it off onto the Earth, for these are the seeds of your legacy that are now rooted deeply. Remember why you are here and the impact you are meant to shine. *You are the Medicine.* Thank Eagle for their support during this journey, and slowly breathe yourself back into your body, this space, as you open your eyes.

Medicine Reflection: What is the legacy you are leaving behind?

CYCLE-BREAKER MEDICINE

If you come from an Ancestral lineage of racial or other forms of trauma, it can be a common experience to feel as though there is an overwhelming amount of work you need to do and cycles of wounding you need to break through to bring freedom to your life and those of your descendants.

My parents are beautiful examples of this. When my father was kicked out of his home at 15, he made a conscious choice at that young age to create a new way. It was a tough road, absent of compassion, love, and privilege, yet today he stands as a proud leader in our Indigenous community. He broke cycles of abuse and is one of the kindest people I know. My mother tells me that when she was pregnant, she was worried that she wouldn't be able to mother well, her own unhealed wounds stoking that fear. Every day of my life, I am deeply grateful for my mother and the unconditional love she poured into me. She broke deep cycles, and the legacy of love, grace, and beauty now flows through the seven generations that will follow her choices to mother me differently. She once told me that if I don't stand with pride in who I am, then all of her intentional healing work will have been lost. In my times of doubt, this pushes me forward. We can all choose to be cycle breakers and carry a vision of a new way. I am breaking down systems of colonization and oppression and choosing liberation, joy, ease, and abundance.

Medicine Reflection: What generational cycles are you breaking?

As a mother myself, I had a harrowing birth experience with my first child that cracked me open in many ways. As I look back, I can see how we both chose to break deep patterns of generational trauma through that experience to pave the way for joy. My eldest is a Healer, through and through, so it doesn't surprise me that his soul chose to co-create this incredible feat with me. After that happened, I began to do healing work around calling in abundance, joy, and flow. I was done with struggle and suffering, for that had been part of my physical experience for most of my life. I began asking myself how I could thrive and be well.

My second child was an unexpected gift and blessing. When he entered my womb space, I had this rush of new energy. I remember buying a banner that said "Time for Joy" and hanging it in our living room. My birth experience was much more positive, and he continues to be a burst of sunshine in our lives. My eldest and I broke massive cycles together. My Indigenous children and I now walk toward ease because of the powerful intentional cycle breakers we came here to be. We are choosing to put an end to suffering and struggling together. We are breaking through all of the limitations that have previously clipped our wings. We can all choose this and finally spread our wings like Eagle. It's not always an easy path, but it's worth it.

THE POWER OF A RIPPLE

When I was running my homeopathic practice, I remember wanting to know how my patients were doing after our work together. Did the remedy I prescribed work? Did they find relief from their symptoms? It was difficult for me when the patient didn't book a follow-up and I never learned the outcome. Self-doubt began creeping in as I worried that, regardless of my training and experience, I may be failing my patients somehow. After being in practice for a few years, I began to receive emails from or occasionally bump into past clients, and they would tell me that working with me changed their lives. Imagine that! All this time, I had been worrying that perhaps what I had offered wasn't helpful; but instead, it was the exact ripple of healing that they needed at that time on their journey.

You make an impact, too! Sometimes you just don't know about it. Maybe a post you made on social media stayed in someone's heart for a long time or maybe it was a card that you sent years ago that the recipient still cherishes. Never underestimate the power that you, showing up as you, has on the world around you. While the feedback may not be immediate, your Medicine ripples could be changing lives. It only takes one voice to impact millions. It only takes one presence to inspire many.

When I hear someone share a compliment or beautiful sentiment about someone who is not present, I make a conscious effort to share it with that person. If I can be a messenger of love to remind someone that their impact matters, I've contributed to building more connection in the world. The more we practice seeing, sharing, and acknowledging the gifts of others, the more ours will be honored, too.

> **Medicine Reflection:** Write an email, note, or card to five people who have impacted your life positively, even if you can't send it for whatever reason. How does that make you feel?

SPIRIT NAME

In our tradition, at some point in our lives, we receive a Spirit Name. Your name is offered to give you a sense of belonging, channeled by a Medicine Person, Elder, or Healer, and it is meant to call your Spirit back home so it may root fully in your body. As your Spirit aligns and fills up all the spaces of self, it calls you to your purpose and offers you direction. It is a great honor to carry a Spirit Name, and the teachings you share from this place impact all of those you touch. When you introduce yourself by your name, you remember that you are guarded by the Ancestors and protected by the Great Spirit. This is who the Ancestors know you by, so as you share it aloud, they recognize you.

Years ago I did a Shamanic journey where we could see what our destiny held for us. I remember the image as clear as day: I was standing in the middle of a field, and I was wearing a beautiful ribbon skirt filled with all the colors of the rainbow. There were children seated around me on the Earth and I was teaching them. Thousands of beads spilled out of my skirt, and the children rushed to gather them. At that time of my life, I was not yet a mother, nor was I teaching anything to anyone. This journey—like all of the journeys I've done in my life—planted a seed in my heart and I let my path unfold.

A few years later, I was sitting on the Land of my Ancestors, *Neyaashiinigmiing*, with my Grandparents on a beautiful sunny day. My in-laws were also there, as were my husband and my mother, my Elder. We lit some smudge, and my *Mishomis* (Grandfather) moved the smoke through his hands. He began to speak in Ojibwe, offering prayers to our Ancestors. A Hawk alighted on a nearby post.

I watched my *Mishomis* listen, I heard him speak words that I couldn't quite translate, but the vibration and sound brought tears to my eyes, a remembering of sorts. When he finished praying, he said to me, "Your name is Healing Rainbow Woman—*Nenaandawi Nagweyaab Kwe*." I remember wondering what it all meant in that moment. I wondered if I could hold this Medicine and make him proud. Tears ran down my face as I felt deeply seen by all of those who had gathered. I vowed to walk with integrity and grace. I promised to rise as my Ancestors asked of me, and I remembered the Destiny Retrieval that I had done all those years ago, when I had a vision of teaching children in that rainbow skirt.

It's been over a decade since I received my Spirit Name, and I have gone through different reflections, expressions, and understandings of it. When I facilitated Medicine work through one-on-one appointments or healing circles, I would see Rainbows energetically coming out of my hands and through my third eye. I would sense Rainbow light coming out of my heart when opening a circle or activating energy during a Ceremony.

Over the last two years, since I wrote my Dear White Woman letter addressing the cultural appropriation of our traditional Ceremonies and teachings, I realized that my understanding of this sacred name that was gifted to me was evolving. I have come to know that I am a bridge between two worlds. I stand as a trailblazer between traditional and modern ways. I walk in balance and harmony, bringing all folks together and helping us move love into action. It has not been easy to be a bridge, one foot in each world, but Spirit moves me to stand firm. And so, I listen, trust, and continue on. It's the only way. My legacy is planted, and I continue to take the steps needed to create ripples for the generations to come.

As I look back to that shamanic journey when I claimed my destiny, I can't help but think of all the forgotten Indigenous children that died in residential schools. I got chills when I realized that the children in my vision are not just my students and clients, but the Spirits of those who didn't get to live out their lives. They are the ones who guide me to share, speak, and rise. They whisper for me to keep going, even when it's hard, for they never had that opportunity. I hand them beads filled with love and compassion. They will be our Elders now. I promise to listen to them in that way, the dancing, bright-eyed, precious Wisdom Keepers in the Cosmos.

My children's Spirit Names also continue to evolve as I get to know them. My eldest's name is Prairie Man (*Mashkode Inini*). He carries the ability to vision and intuit, seeing far and wide. Recently I have seen how he carries deep Buffalo Spirit Medicine—the Animal that roamed the prairies—as he has a generous heart and helps people feel held and safe. My youngest is Chief of the Good Road (*Ogaamaawi Mino-Bimaadizi),* which makes me smile, as since he's been here, we have called him "Boss Baby." It is a true privilege that I, an Indigenous Mother, get to tuck my babies in at night and nurture them in my home, something that many Indigenous parents never had the opportunity to do.

Medicine Reflection: What does your given name mean? Does it inform the way you show up in the world?

TRUE LEADERSHIP

The Eagle is the leader of the birds. It says that this is what it means to be a good leader, to have vision, to be generous . . . It reminds the whole community that leadership is not rooted in power and authority but in service and wisdom.

— ROBIN WALL KIMMERER, *Braiding Sweetgrass*

The gift of studying with many Healers and teachers is that I have been able to witness how different people lead, guide, and mentor. Some of my biggest learning lessons have come from uncomfortable or even abusive situations with varying teachers in my life. Even though they were extremely challenging, these situations helped me see the harm that comes from leading without accountability.

Checking in with those who will hold you to your integrity is of great importance. I am not perfect in any way and have made mistakes, too. But what I learned from experiencing harmful leadership is that I will always have a strong team of therapists, supervisors, and Healers so that I will always be doing my healing work alongside those who work with me. This doesn't safeguard us from messing up—we are human, after all—but at least we can walk in repair as we heal ourselves and continue to build trust with those we are in a relationship with.

I believe that we can all be leaders in some way. When I say this in my mentorship circles, I notice people start to squirm in discomfort, and understandably so. Leadership has had some unfavorable connotations, often modeled with top-down force or hierarchical weight. Leaders of governments all over the world have often been violent and abusive. Leaders hold great responsibility, so I understand why some shrink away from this burden. I believe that leadership can begin in our own heart, and we can choose to walk with grace, integrity, or any other way we choose, as we guide.

Ask yourself the following to dig deeper into the question of how you are leading in your own life:

1. What are the top three values that you hold most dear?

2. What do you feel you have healed through in your life that you now share as wisdom with others?

3. What do you want to model to those around you or the next generation?

4. What communities do you impact? (Remember that your own family, kin, or friendship relationships are communities, too!)

Vision Quest

Years ago, I set out on a Vision Quest with a Medicine Person. A Vision Quest can be done in various ways, but this time we incorporated what is called a fast, as you go without food and water for the time you are on the Land. At the time, I was pretty burnt out in my private practice and wondering what was to come. This time on the Land is devoted to listening to Spirit and all of Creation. I remember receiving guidance that things couldn't go on as they have been, that I needed to find a more sustainable way of sharing my Medicine with the world. I saw the Spirit of my eldest son, who was my only child then, planting his seeds as I planted mine. I thought about the legacy that I would leave behind for him and all the steps he would take. I knew that I wanted to be fully present for it all. Something needed to change.

At the moment where I felt extremely thirsty and overheated by the Sun, two Eagles circled above my head. When I asked what message they had to share with me, they asked me to rise into my leadership, reminding me that it is in my blood to lead with grace, reciprocity, and vision. They reminded me what that psychic had told me: I was the teacher, the example. My descendants would be rooting their Medicine Walk into the Earth based on how I chose to show up for mine. They gave me wings, they gave me insight, and most importantly, they showed me that it was possible for me to soar. And so, I did.

I began to create more sustainable options for my business and started to dream of a global community where I would share Medicine, healing, Ceremony, and teachings. To this day, I believe that those Eagles guided me to this Creation. I took a leap of faith, knowing that every step of the way, I was leaving behind a legacy that would one day inspire the generations to come.

A Gift of Feathers

One day, the same Medicine Person that held space with me for my Vision Quest told me that they had a gift for me. They had found an Eagle on the side of the road and brought it into their sweat lodge to honor it. The Eagle offered them feathers, and they gifted me with seven. I felt so blessed and didn't quite know what I had done to earn these feathers, but I received them with deep gratitude. Eagle feathers are gifted to us when we are being called to lead in some way, as a Healer, Medicine Person, or Wisdom Keeper. I had received one on my wedding day from my Father, and this gift of seven felt very sacred. To me, they represented the seven generations of healing that I think about every day as I walk gently upon this Earth. Each feather reminds me that the words I speak, the steps I walk, and the healing I do will impact many. The ripples will reach far wider than I can even imagine. Such a gift that I received that day, one I carry into my leadership with pride.

Eagle Medicine Invocation

Dearest Eagle, thank you for my wings. I promise to honor them and listen to how I'm being called to rise. Thank you for helping me remember my big vision. I invite you into my body, my heart, my soul. Remind me of why I am here and what I am meant to do to serve the world. Thank you for helping me align with my most potent self. I commit to rising into leadership and walking my path in my own way. I am grateful for your reminder that my legacy matters.

Mdaamiin Giizis Moon Affirmation

With every intentional action I take, I am conscious about the impact I make on the future generations, the Earth, and my Kin. My legacy matters and I create ripples of love with my intentional flight. I am the Medicine.

CHAPTER 11

BIINAAKWE GIIZIS
FALLING LEAVES
MOON

Our tenth Moon of Creation occurs in October and shares the gift of autumn in the Northern Hemisphere. The leaves change and turn the most vibrant colors, and an abundance of beauty surrounds us. The Trees share teachings with us about the miracles that happen before our very eyes and remind us of the Earth's cycles. We, too, go through cycles daily, monthly, and yearly, and when we deepen into those cycles, we find peace. This Moon reminds us that when we surrender, release, and let things die, we make room for glorious things to enter.

Moon Legend: How the Buffalo Found Beauty in Death

There was a time when Buffalo were plentiful and roamed free across the Land. The Land was abundant and expansive, and they would migrate in huge herds.

Buffalo was a dear friend of the First People, and they had great respect for this Animal. The people who lived on the plains depended on Buffalo for their survival; their relationship was essential. The two coexisted in recipro-cal ways. The people treated the Buffalo as the precious Kin they were, using almost every part of them to survive. They offered gratitude daily for all Buffalo offered them, and Buffalo was honored to do so.

One day the dark force of colonization took over the Land. There was a time when the oppressive forces wanted to get rid of the First Peoples who lived on the plains. This was the same dark force that had sent the children to residential schools and given diseases to the First Peo-ple. They wanted to extinguish the First People, and they knew that one way to do this was to wipe out the Buffalo.

The dark forces did this in horrible and disrespectful ways, burning the dead Buffalo so that the First People could not use any part of them to support their way of life. Thousands of Buffalo were dying at a time, and the First People were devastated by the loss. Buffalo was almost extinguished completely, but much like the First Peoples, their Spirits were resilient. They trusted that there was a reason for their deaths and, as thousands of their Spirits soared to the Stars, they left their friends, the First Peo-ples, a sign of hope that one day they would make a come-back and roam the Earth again.

They decided to make the Stars shine brighter than anyone had ever seen before; the constellations had never been so colorful! From the Stars, they offered and blessed the First Peoples; they sent prayers for protection and abundance to their Kin. From that day forward, the Spirit of Buffalo reminded us all that there is beauty to be found in letting go.

Animal Spirit: *Mashkode Bizhiki* (Buffalo)

The Animal Spirit that best represents our tenth Moon of Creation is Buffalo, or as they are known in Anishiinabe-mowin, *Mashkode Bizhiki*. Buffalo Medicine is one of powerful support, liberation, and abundance. It can be challenging to let go of that which weighs heavy on our hearts, minds, and spirits, but Buffalo is here for us to lean into as we do. Buffalo reminds us that we are worthy of abundance, and when we clear out the old, we make room for what is meant for us. Buffalo comes in as an ally for liberation, helping us to free ourselves of our past limitations. They gather around us energetically to provide us with solid and secure footing and infuse us with trust. We can rest in the love and safety of Buffalo that all will be well as we release the layers that need to go. This Animal Medicine reminds us that we are worthy of receiving abundance in all forms; we are worthy of this deep support.

Buffalo Message

- It's safe to let go.
- Death is sacred.
- Releasing makes room.
- Abundance is your birthright.

The trees are about to show us how
lovely it is to let things go.

— UNKNOWN

THAT FEELING

We all know when something begins to weigh heavily on our heart, body, and Spirit. For some, it is a sensory experience, perhaps a feeling of oppression in the chest or unsettledness in the gut. For others, it might be a constant cycle of overthinking, of not knowing where to go or what to do next. It might be a feeling of anxiety that something needs to change, but we can't put our finger on exactly what that is. This state of heaviness can feel confusing; we don't know where we are going, yet we know that something needs to be addressed, acknowledged, and felt. It can be uncomfortable to come to terms with something that needs to be released. Perhaps we have stuffed those feelings down for some time simply to survive. There is no shame in this. These feelings, sensations, and thoughts will continue to persist until we have the courage to truly look at them. When we allow the truth to flood our system, clarity begins to rise. When it's time to let something die, it's time. Just like the leaves that change color and fall to the Earth, or the Plants and Flowers that succumb to the first frost, we must trust the inherent life cycle that pulses through all of Creation and release what is no longer thriving.

> **Medicine Reflection:** Is there anything weighing you down that needs to be acknowledged today?

IT'S SAFE TO FEEL

Giving ourselves expansive space and time to feel our experiences, challenges, and struggles fully and deeply has not been valued or encouraged in modern culture. We get messages like "Get over it," "Stop crying," "It could be worse," or "Vulnerability is weakness." This leads us to try to process things as quickly as possible to jump into "fixing mode" and find a solution. Or we suppress, shut down, and invalidate all that we are experiencing. Think about a time when someone sat with you and held a beautiful space for your heart and feelings. What was it about their presence that felt validating?

Here are some offerings of love—statements that can help the receiver feel held and seen:

- "I see you."
- "That's understandable."
- "I'm sorry that happened to you."
- "I'm here to hold space for you and listen."

There is no attempt to fix or offer solutions in these statements; there is just sacred, conscious, and loving space. If you haven't had the experience of someone holding this space for you, I believe you can hold it for yourself. Try saying these statements to parts of you that have not felt seen, or repeat them at times when your emotions got locked in or stuck. May you feel safe to let them flow and be seen.

No Good-byes

Learning to surrender can be a spiritual practice in itself. I, for one, have not mastered it in this lifetime and, for most of my life, I struggled with letting go. My hands, my arms, and my heart hold on to people, situations, business offerings, and emotions for dear life, even if by holding on I am dragging myself down. It's hard for me to say good-bye. We do not have a word for "good-bye" in our Anishinaabe language, instead we say *"baamaapii,"* which can be translated "see you again." My interpretation of this is that there are no final good-byes. Life is a continuous, ever-flowing circle. When something important enters our lives, whether it be a relationship, a career, or even an emotion, we will continue to feel its influence, even after it leaves. The more we are in touch with the natural ebb and flow of these impactful people and forces in our lives, the less suffering we will have.

You may have experienced the Medicine of *baamaapii* before in your relationships. In death, our loved ones may come back as an Animal; alternatively, when a relationship comes to an end, those people may come back to us in our dreams. An old friend may come back into your life after a long hiatus. The presence of the people in our lives, no matter how brief, has the potential to impact us for a lifetime. For me, those whose paths have diverged from mine have left a unique imprint on my being forever. I bless them all, for there are no good-byes. Our Spirits are connected. I will see them again.

RELEASING CONSCIOUSLY

Letting go in a conscious and healthy way is not something that is modeled to us in our modern times. Social media demonstrates this to us daily as we "cancel" people, thoughts, and ideas, and block relationships that never had a chance to heal. I get it—it's painful to feel, process, and acknowledge—and while I'm all for setting boundaries when needed, I wonder what our world would be like with more space for nuance and repair. When something feels as though it's coming to an end, we either deny it or rush through it so that we can feel relief. Cutting things off, speeding through the process, and not allowing the space something needs to end or die keeps us from integrating precious wisdom. Breakdowns, endings, and death are all vital aspects of the cycle of Creation. When we move through it with the pace and acknowledgment it deserves, we can then move to the next cycle, liberated and free.

One lesson I've learned about letting go is that you can still love something or someone and release them from your life. I learned this lesson with my private practice. I started it when I was 27 and poured every inch of love, Medicine, and support into the thousands of folks I saw over the years. Eight years in, after the birth of my first child, I started to get messages from Spirit and my heart that I was meant to evolve this practice into something new. This terrified me, quite honestly, as it had become steady, rooted, and comfortable, and I didn't know what this next iteration of my work would look like. Those little nudges from above and within signaled to me that the process of letting go had begun. It was a slow process. I continued seeing patients and facilitating circles the way I had been for another few years, and the nudges got louder. I began to receive clear visions around where I was going, yet I didn't know how I would get there with everything on my plate. I held space for 16 to 20 patients per week and offered circles a few times per month. My plate was full; there was no way I could add in something new.

It was then that I received the wisdom that is there for all of us when we listen: I needed to let go of what felt safe and secure to make room for where Spirit was guiding me. I loved my private practice and I loved every one of my clients; they had taught me so much in those years of service. But my heart and gut said it was time. So many people told me I was making a mistake and that there was no way people would follow me to my next dream. Ultimately, I had to trust myself and what was best for me. This was a challenging journey for the people-pleaser in me, but one that has shown me that beauty is at the other end of letting go.

The Space In Between

Once you have let go of something, you stand in that space in between. Letting go of secure and familiar things can feel disorienting. It is here where I hear people say, "I feel so lost. I don't know where I am going." You are in this expansive void of the unknown, and it can feel like you are spinning through space, untethered. Nothing new has had the chance to fill up the emptiness quite yet, and so you search for footing. Even if you have ideas, intentions, or dreams about what you might want to fill it with, if you are too rigidly attached to your plans, you don't leave room for the magic waiting to flow through. This place may feel slow and unproductive, yet you must trust. Insecurities will rise, and you must allow them. This space in between is where I see people "leap out" too early, rush through to get to the next thing, and abandon the space. I've done it, too. Whenever you rush into something, it ends up being a short-lived solution—ultimately, this lesson will come around again.

This liminal space is a rite of passage, where the fire is burning everything away and all that we are left with are the ashes. I have learned that there is less suffering if we can let those ashes fall to the Earth and sink into the Medicine of the in-between, for it is a space where deep wisdom flows. A few years ago, I attended a self-care retreat with the author Cheryl Richardson, and she said something that struck me deeply: "Your meandering has purpose." I will always remember this when I feel lost, disoriented, or confused about which way my path is leading me. The insecurity and swirling vortex of the space in between has a purpose.

> **Medicine Reflection:** In what ways do you know that a cycle is complete?

BARRIERS TO TRUST

We have all heard variations of these inspirational quotes: "This is not happening *to* you; it's happening *for* you," "What is meant for you will not pass you by," "Everything happens for a reason," and many others. In theory these quotes are a beautiful thing to believe, embody, and live, yet we struggle. These quotes simplify our lived experience and minimize how patriarchal, colonial, and systemic oppression have impacted certain groups more than others. This is a fundamental distinction to make when offering these platitudes to marginalized folks such as the LGBTQ+ community, BIPOC, people who live with chronic conditions, or anyone else not living with certain privileges in a way that impacts their ability to trust, surrender, manifest, or call in abundance. The truth is, the system has created barriers; we cannot bypass this reality, so this is not a one-size-fits-all approach.

I wish that we could address the systemic issues that plague our society in a day, but we all know that this is an impossible feat. So, we must focus on what we *can* do. This is where our healing work can come in to support us in dismantling and unweaving the impacts of systemic damage, cultural conditioning, and Ancestral trauma.

Here are some examples of how trauma can manifest and impact a person's ability to trust or surrender:

- Ancestral trauma around Land or home being taken away through settler contact, war, political issues, natural disasters, government initiatives, slavery, indentured servitude, or other issues.

- Lack of equitable opportunities due to racism, white supremacy, and systems of oppression.

- Abandonment or abuse by a parental figure or loved one resulting in a lack of secure attachment.

- Not having basic needs met—famine, poverty, starvation, homelessness.

- Past-life memories.

Clearly it's not as easy as "trust, and you shall receive," but know there is potential for every one of us to acknowledge, feel into, and heal our own trauma in a supportive, healthy way so that we can begin to feel safe to surrender. Sometimes we need to let go of what feels safe and secure to allow what is meant for us to be birthed, even if it's scary, painful, or takes some intentional work.

Medicine Reflection: What (if anything) prevents you from fully being able to surrender and trust?

MEDICINE JOURNEY
Surrendering with the Ancestors and Buffalo

Find a comfortable space to sit or lie down, and welcome in Buffalo and your Ancestors. Pay attention to your breath. Your Ancestors who were Healers step forward. You feel a sense of great comfort and security as they hold the mastery we need to clear and heal today. Buffalo stands at their side, offering support and expansive love.

A Medicine Person steps forward, dressed in the traditional clothing of your Ancestors, and asks you the following questions:

"What are you holding on to that you know you must release?"

"Look down at your hands. How tight is your grasp upon this thing?"

"Feel into your heart. Is there any emotion around letting go? What rises for you?"

They lead you to a great fire, and you see it's flickering with all the colors of the rainbow. This is a transformative fire, one that can clear lifetimes of Ancestral, collective, and even past-life trauma. It is potent and powerful. You are drawn to step into it. Feel the warmth and the colorful flames dancing through your energetic field. Buffalo stands beside you, holding space and reminding you that you have come so far. You have walked, carrying this trauma, for so long, and it's not your fault you have not been able to set it down. The fire acknowledges all the past and present pain in you and your Ancestors, validating the depth of trauma you have witnessed and carried. Buffalo reminds you to let go of anything you are ready to release in this moment. Sometimes, surrendering a little bit at a time, piece by piece, is what is needed.

As the fire moves through your system, your hands relax and uncurl, your breathing deepens as your chest opens, and your nervous system settles as you feel Buffalo's Medicine pour over and into you. Release, release, release. The Healer continues to work their energy through your system and your Ancestors gather in full support. Know that the healing work that you have done today blesses those generations behind you and those to come. You are creating a space of liberation for your lineage, for yourself, and for the future.

As you step out of the fire, you continue to be surrounded by rainbow light. One ribbon of color stands out to you, and you feel it wrapping around you like a cloak or robe. This color will remind you that it's safe to trust every time you see or wear it. *You are the Medicine.* Slowly and gently bring yourself back to your body and the space you are in, thanking your Ancestors and Buffalo for their support.

THE MEDICINE OF ABUNDANCE

I have this vision of my people, Indigenous Kin, walking with, surrounded in, and fed by abundance. It's a vision that predates colonization and settler contact. My vision shows us honoring reciprocal giving and receiving, living in community and supporting one another, offering our deepest gifts and Medicines to one another, and being nourished in all ways.

I've even had this dream of standing on the shores of the Georgian Bay where my Ancestors lived and breathed. With open arms and open hearts, they welcomed those who were coming in boats, trusting that they had good intentions and were here to build honorable relationships. As we know now, reciprocal and ethical relationships between Indigenous people and settlers did not happen. It brings me deep grief to think that the light of abundance for my people was extinguished in so many ways.

Because I know that this memory of abundance lives in my blood and bones, I stand for reclaiming it for myself, my Ancestors, and the generations to come. We all have different definitions of abundance. For me, abundance means that I am surrounded by love, health, friendship, beauty, spaciousness, and food, shelter, and time to heal. Wealth is often taught as a central aspect of abundance, yet capitalism has distorted the meaning of wealth, making it synonymous with greed. Resources are not shared equitably in this system of haves and have-nots, and so much damage has been done to our Kin, the Land, and Creation by the hands that hold the majority of the wealth in this world.

I wonder how that could shift if money were in the hands of those who were conscious and responsible stewards of it? Imagine a world where those who care deeply about the Earth and all our Kin held more monetary wealth. So many people are already living with values of reciprocity, gratitude, balance, and generosity as guiding principles in their lives. I guarantee resources would be shared and not hoarded. I am confident that if wealth were distributed through different hands we would find equitable and reciprocal ways to uplift and change the way money flows around our planet.

I envision myself as a channel for wealth and other forms of abundance to flow through. It's a never-ending flow and I intentionally direct where that energy goes. I am not a sinkhole, trapping all the resources; I am an open channel in relationship with all of Creation, giving, receiving, and redistributing resources where needed. I hope you will dream this into reality with me.

Medicine Reflection: What does abundance mean to you?

MONEY MEDICINE

As I shared earlier, before colonization, Indigenous people traditionally lived in communities where we took care of one another. Everyone made sure each member of the group was fed, warm, and well. Medicine People were always taken care of when offering healing or Ceremony to their tribe. They were feasted and showered with all that they needed. Money didn't change hands in the way it does today, but the trading of goods and services was standard. Traditionally, we were gifted with Tobacco as a form of gratitude and honor for the Medicine work we offered. This was a mutually sustainable way of life for all.

Today, things are much different. Nobody is offering me furs for my children to wear or delivering me food to feed my family in exchange for my healing Medicine. There are no offers of a warm home for me to live in or a bed to rest my head on at night. This has been an issue of contention at times with my work in the world. Since our traditional ways state that Medicine People only receive Tobacco for their healing, I have heard that true Healers don't accept money. I have heard that it's greedy and selfish and that you don't carry a true "gift" if you receive money for it.

Years ago, I started to notice that the Medicine People I was working with couldn't afford to buy shoes or provide for their families. These Medicine People were creating miraculous healing and serving the community, yet they couldn't afford to buy the clothes they needed for comfort or pay the rent to provide a safe home for their children. This seemed unfair and not in right relation to their worth. I knew then that we were not meant to struggle in this way—but I also understood how hard it was to root into our worth and ask for what we are owed.

That same year I noticed that there were Healers who were dying early. They were brilliant at what they did, but they weren't here anymore to share their gifts or live to a ripe old age. I couldn't help but wonder if they burned out their vital force by being overly generous with their gifts without receiving generosity in return.

These experiences had me asking myself what I wanted for my life. I, too, was an over-giver—offering a lot for free or giving away my Medicine—and I often ended up burnt out with an empty cup at the end of the day. We are a sharing people, so this came very naturally for me, but something about it was no longer sitting right with me. I struggled with rising into my truth around receiving money as an Indigenous Healer in fear that I would be reprimanded or shamed by my communities. But I came to believe that one of the ways we fill our cups is by receiving money. Money is a form of energy, after all, and it carries its own vital force.

In claiming my right to receive in exchange for all that I give, I also claimed my vision of a long life. I want to see my children and grandchildren thrive. Monetary abundance is my birthright! I desire to have more than enough to take care of my family, and I dream of living by the ocean one day. I have realized that I can be a responsible steward of money and be a channel to distribute it equitably. The reclamation of the abundance that I know my Ancestors hold in their bone memory is part of mine, too. I receive this abundance through the modern currency of money and stand for all people being paid well for the Medicine they share with the world.

> **Medicine Reflection:** How is your relationship with money? If money were a person, how would you relate and speak to it?

HEALERS AND MONEY

As I mentioned, I have worked with many Healers over the years and have found that it is a challenge for them to ask to be paid well for their Medicine gifts. We have been conditioned with the notion that Healers must give selflessly to the community and not be compensated appropriately. Why is our Medicine any less valuable than that of a plumber, a lawyer, or a medical doctor? The gifts that we share with the world are life changing. The possibility of tremendous transformation is vast when we work with a Healer. Vision, space holding, intuition, healing activation, and other gifts are precious. We have every right to claim our value monetarily if we so choose. When we don't have a clear and healthy relationship with receiving money, we create unstable situations around boundaries. We end up facing burnout and a lack of reciprocity for our Medicine gifts.

People will ask for energy, Medicine, advice, and anything else that they feel they need from Healers all the time. They are worthy of being paid for it all. When you are a Healer, it's your time, your energy, and your vital force that you are offering. For me, one of my best uses of money is to pay other incredible Healers, space holders, and Medicine People to help me fill my cup back up, guide me through my blind spots, and help me to evolve to become more masterful at my craft. Money enables me to support the causes close to my heart, giving back to communities and honoring other creators in their work in the world. Money is the energy that assists in keeping me well so that I can move my Medicine out into the world and have a more significant impact. Step into the field of abundance with me. I will be here with open arms.

Reciprocity

Indigenous People have always inherently respected and given back to the Earth. We are taught to walk with gratitude, reverence, and reciprocity in our relationships with the Plants, Trees, Waters, and Animals, yet we can also apply this to our relationships with other humans. I love the practice of blessing all things: people, relationships, challenging interactions, or situations included. When I bless everything that comes my way, I instantly feel that I move into a state where I can give and receive in a balanced way.

Walking in reciprocal ways with all of Creation is an essential part of carrying an abundance mind-set. While money is not the only way to offer reciprocity, we must be mindful of what we take from the Earth and each other. Walking with a state of gratitude and offering to give back for what you have received is a way to walk in right relationship with all our Kin. Be mindful of reciprocity with those guiding you, facilitating healing for you, and offering their Medicine to you. Pay for emotional, physical, and spiritual labor in your learning, especially when you are learning from those who have been historically oppressed, for they have been invisible and devalued for too long. If we all lived in a reciprocal way, the flow of abundance would begin to cut through the systems and structures that keep us down. Gratitude is the gateway for abundance. Practice mindfulness, share, give back, and walk with grace. If we all walked in this Indigenous way, our Earth would heal.

Buffalo Medicine Invocation

Dearest Buffalo, help me continue releasing all that is taking up space in my energy field, heart, and life. Remind me that it is safe to let things die when they have completed their cycle. Shower your Medicine of abundance throughout my life, reminding me of my innate worthiness. I welcome in your teachings that I will always be well taken care of; help me to trust that it is so. Your Medicine now surrounds me, and I am grateful that I can lean into your warm, comforting fur and body at any time.

Biinaakwe Giizis Moon Affirmation

All things move through natural cycles. Just like the leaves on the trees and the plants on the Earth, it is safe to let things go through death. As I release, I make room for what is meant to touch my life. When I acknowledge what has come to an end, I let go and find abundance waiting for me. I am taken care of, always. I am the Medicine.

CHAPTER 12

MSHKAWJI GIIZIS **FREEZING MOON**

Our eleventh Moon of Creation occurs in October when the Star Nations, the Cosmos, and the support from the Upper Worlds are near. With the Star Nations close, sensitivity and intuition are heightened, and all our senses are on alert. Our energy fields are highly attuned during this Moon cycle, so we learn how to protect our dreams, energy, and hearts. Energetic boundaries are an essential part of Creation, and this Moon reminds us that the more we are aware of the impact of our thoughts, actions, and intentions, the more we can walk in alignment with our great vision. The Stars are here to support our well-being, and they wrap us in protection and love.

MOON LEGEND: WHY THE STAR NATIONS CAME CLOSER TO THE EARTH

On the very first Autumn cycle, the cold began to blanket the Earth. The Plants had all gone to sleep, the Trees had lost their leaves, and the Animals were gathering food for the Winter. The Sky at night was deepening into darkness as the freeze began to cover the Land. With the Sky so dark, the Stars shone brighter than ever before. The Stars enjoyed how they could see wide and far from up above. They felt deeply connected to their Earth Kin, even though they were so far away.

One night they looked down from the Upper Worlds and felt shocked. The Animals seemed to be moving very slowly, and the Earth had become so brown, as though everything had died. The Stars wondered what had happened to all the color and life in the Middle World. They were scared and gathered in a meeting to consult with one another. "Maybe there was a great fire!" said the powerful constellation *Gitchi Mkwa* (Big Bear). "Or maybe a great plague has taken over the Earth," said *Wabiizi* (Swan). The nervous chatter of the Stars was so loud it could be heard on the Earth plane. "We need to go down to offer our fierce protection," they said. "We need our Earth Kin to know that we stand by them."

One of the Stars that sat in the constellation *Ma-iingan* (Wolf) had an idea. "I am going to go and visit the Earth and see what's happening!" The others, deeply curious, felt the call in their hearts to join the journey. The next day, they told the Sky that they would be leaving to visit with Earth plane to see what was happening to their Kin. The Sky agreed to let them go and told them that all they had to do was make a wish, and they would find themselves taking a journey down to Earth.

When darkness came, the Star journeyers closed their eyes, activated their hearts, and made a wish to the Cosmos. One by one, they leaped from their home, creating the most beautiful Stardust behind them. It was as though they were soaring and illuminating the night Sky with their magic for all to see—shooting star magnificence. When they reached the Earth, they asked the Plants,

Trees, and Animals what was happening and shared why they had come and their concerns. "Much like you, we move through our own seasons and life cycles, dear Stars. Death, letting go, and hibernation are an important part of renewal." The Stars began to understand and asked if there was anything they could provide to help with this cycle. "Dearest Stars, there are times we feel vulnerable and in need of protection. May we ask you for that?" The Stars agreed and promised to visit the Earth as shooting Stars to deliver extra protection and support when needed.

When it was time for the Stars to return home, they called on their Nations to come closer so that they could journey back. Creator offered a trail of Stardust to the beings, and they floated up to the Cosmos. Every year during this Moon cycle, the Star Nations come closer so that they can visit with their Kin and, in doing so, offer safety to them during the time of freezing. The veil thins, the pathways to our Ancestors and Guides open, and we are able to intuit, sense, and vision more deeply.

Animal Spirit: *Ma'iingan* (Wolf)

The Animal Spirit that best represents our eleventh Moon of Creation is the Wolf, or as they are known in Anishiinabemowin, *Ma'iingan.* As Wolf howls to the Upper Worlds, they help to call down the healing energies needed to support our path and evolution. Wolf is a guardian and protector who carries the Medicine of energetic boundaries and provides us with protection. Fierce in their Medicine, Wolf is part of our support pack as we need them. Wolf carries strong instincts and can remind us of how our sensitivity and intuition can be used to "track" the energy in our lives. They encourage us to listen to our senses more deeply, trust what we are receiving, and take bold action when needed.

Wolf will walk with us and growl to help guard our space. This Medicine safeguards our sacred resources, preserves our vitality, and heals our lives.

Wolf Message

- Protection is all around.
- Self-preservation is vital to your healing.
- Howl at the Moon and Stars; they are listening.
- Engage all of your senses.

TRACKING

The concept of "tracking" was introduced to me by an Algonquin Medicine Healer who held the ability to see the root of an issue and bring it forward. At the time, I was already engaging in this Medicine in my homeopathic and healing practice, but I didn't have a name for it. In homeopathy school, our teachers would tell us that the first question to ask after taking case notes was "What needs to be healed?" We were to discern what was coming to the forefront. To be a successful practitioner, tracking skills are necessary. Like Wolf, we use our refined senses to notice what is calling us to see, hear, feel, taste, smell, or know. I remember the Algonquin Medicine Healer describing Wolf Medicine and how Wolf carries this profound ability to track energy. I got chills knowing that this is what I had been doing, and now I would be able to amplify and grow my abilities through learning with him. Tracking involves using all your senses to gain clarity and discover what is calling for healing in each patient. When we do this through the lens of unconditional love and compassion, we aren't looking for what's wrong; instead, we see all that is divine first and foremost and then help the other parts remember their innate nature.

My osteopath once described this beautifully, stating that he places his hands upon the body and feels into the perfection of that body and sees all the parts that are working well and in good health; this is where he begins. His mission is to next gently, compassionately, and lovingly call all the other parts into this state, trusting that the body and Spirit can go there. This is a profoundly sacred way to treat our systems and one that I aspire to daily in my work.

Medicine Reflection: Do you feel you are able to track energy? What senses are most pronounced when you do this?

YOUR ESSENCE IS PRECIOUS

As a child, I remember feeling what everyone around me was feeling. I was highly sensitive and empathic. I could sense what they weren't saying, feel the emotions they weren't expressing, and I felt like I absorbed all that heaviness into my body. I didn't know about boundaries, protection, or how to preserve my energy at that point. I was a Medicine Person in training, even way back then; I was hypervigilant to the needs of those around me even at that young age, an emotional shapeshifter of sorts, becoming what those around me needed me to be. Love is everything to a child. If we are not receiving the love and attention that we deserve, we find ways to get it, and for me, it was by being as "good" as I could be. I pleased everyone around me and made sure that everyone was okay—even those whose job was to make sure I was okay. Coming to this life with a soul purpose as a Healer and peaceful warrior also contributed to how I showed up in the world. I wanted to help; I wanted to shift the energy for all so that we could return to harmony. It was a huge responsibility for a child that I put on myself and one that I've had to work to let go. I now know I can only be responsible for *my* energy, a lesson that has come with an enormous learning curve.

Someone once asked me, "Do you feel that your energy is precious and deserves to be taken care of?" There was something about the word "precious" that brought tears to my eyes. My immediate answer was no; I didn't feel worthy of being cared for or protected, nor did I feel precious. This experience affirmed for me why my boundaries were so porous and why it was such a growth edge for me to uphold them for myself.

In my experience, people who are sensitive souls or identify as Healers tend to:

- Fill the role of nurturer in their family system.
- Be conditioned to value others more highly than themselves.
- Lean toward people-pleasing and have a hard time saying no.
- Take on energy that is not theirs to hold.
- Carry the weight of the world in their bodies and auric fields.

They also tend to be the ones who are breaking the cycles of familial and Ancestral patterns, turning trauma into wisdom and alchemizing pain into Medicine. Focusing on others first and walking with deep sensitivity and empathy can leave us wide open to all sorts of energy. Some energies are helpful and supportive; others not so much. To lean into the truth that our bodies, hearts, and spirits are precious and deserve care is essential to thriving in this world.

Medicine Reflection: Do you see your essence as precious and worthy of being taken care of? Why or why not?

ENERGY FIELD

Each one of us has an energetic field in the form of a vibrational pulse that surrounds our body. It interacts with all the systems of our mind, body, and Spirit. It also interacts with the outer world, other people, and outside forces. If you rub your hands together for a few seconds and then pull them apart, you will begin to feel the essence of this type of energy. There are different theories on how far your energetic field extends. Some say that if you were to stretch your arms out to the side and "draw" an egg shape around your body from head to toe, that is the extent of your field. Others feel that it is vast and infinite and can stretch and shrink as needed. What is most important is to identify how it feels in your system so that you can work with it. Our energy field directly relates to our boundaries, and it can be rigid, porous, or somewhere in between. There is no "perfect" energy field just as there is more than one way to exist in the world. Nor is our energy field static; it shifts and evolves as we move through our journey.

Wherever you are along the spectrum from porous to rigid, your state reflects precisely what you've needed in your life. Our energetic field can be impacted by familial, Ancestral, past life, and collective energies. In building a deeper relationship with our fields, we may feel the call to move to a more neutral place. Our system always knows, and the most important thing is awareness. There is no shame or judgment here; we are simply observing. I believe that we can always move toward what our system needs most for our healing; we get to choose.

MEDICINE JOURNEY
Energy Field Awareness

Find a comfortable space to sit or lie down, and begin to breathe. Welcome in Wolf Spirit. You see a golden door appear and you begin to walk through. Wolf pads along at your side, and you feel the presence of your body with every step. They lead you to a sacred clearing that has been prepared for you, and the Stars have all gathered here to hold space. Wolf starts to howl at the Stars, and the sound vibrates through your whole body. You notice that you can feel, sense, and see more deeply. Stretch your arms up to the Sky and move them down as though you are drawing a bubble around you. Are there any textures, sensations, colors? Are there any breaks or tears? What about any objects or images? Wolf guards your space as you do this.

Wolf begins to growl, activating their tracking abilities, and the vibration of this shakes up your energy field, clearing out anything that might be harming or impacting you. Allow yourself to be purified as the Star Nations begin to wash you with starlight. A waterfall of this energy flows over you. You are now fully present with your natural energy field.

Stand rooted to the Earth, and as one with the Stars, and ask your Spirit, "Is my energy field more porous or rigid?"

Ask your Spirit to show you, on a scale of 1 to 10, how porous your energy field is. If your field is porous, it might need stability, mending, and security.

Ask your Spirit to show you, on a scale of 1 to 10, how rigid your energy field is. If your field is rigid, it might need softening, gentleness, and trust.

Wolf creates a powerful, clear boundary around your field by walking around it in a clockwise circle. They offer you what you need; let it inform your energy field and be open to the healing continuing to flow for the days to come. They complete their work with a loud howl to the Stars, and your energy field shines with illumination. *You are the Medicine.* Wolf walks with you, back to the path, back to the door, and before you exit, you take a moment to feel the difference in your system. You are now standing in your power. Breathe yourself back, slowly and gently, and when you feel ready, open your eyes.

Medicine Reflection: What did the journey tell you about your energy field?

PROTECTION

We are constantly interacting with different vibrations, subtle transmissions, and frequencies in our daily lives. It is to our advantage to be mindful of the frequencies that we bring into spaces, the energy we immerse ourselves in, and the thoughts we send out consciously and unconsciously. As a Healer and Medicine Person, I have been gifted many opportunities to practice, engage with, and learn about protection. Energy has an impact, and the Freezing Moon teachings us that the more we tend to our systems, the more impeccable we can be with how we wield it, care for it, and share it with the world.

There are many helpers both in the physical and Spirit Worlds that can offer us protection. You might have experienced calling on Archangels or certain Animal Spirits to help with this, or maybe your Ancestors are beings that provide this for you. Many Plant Medicines also offer protection for different aspects of our body, mind, and Spirit. Plants that we develop a sacred relationship with can be worn in our Medicine Bundle, placed on our altar, taken in a tincture or flower essence, or burned as Smoke Medicine. As discussed in chapter 5 about cleansing and purification, Plants that connect you to your lineage and ancestry will always be the most powerful.

These helpers, whether Spirit, Angel, Animal, or Plant, provide effective ways to surround ourselves with protection. However, what I have found to be valid for both myself and my clients is that these protection allies work best when you combine them with your inner healing work. If we don't go to the root and heal through why energies impact us, these practices become temporary solutions. Therefore, a combination of your inner work and calling in protection allies is truly the best way.

Reasons you might feel the need for protection:

- Jealousy or envy is directed your way.

- Energies are draining you.

- You find yourself carrying other people's emotions and heaviness.

- You feel exhausted and have no reason to feel that way.

- Your capacity is low.

- You feel vulnerable.

To get to the root of where energy leaks are occurring, we must be honest with ourselves. An energy leak is simply something that we have not yet brought consciousness to. Once we see it, we can meet it with love, compassion, and healing.

An energy leak could be from:

- a tendency to say yes when you mean no.

- not listening to your body when you need to rest.

- people-pleasing.
- trying to rescue or enable others.
- codependency in relationships.

I believe that the best protection comes from the inside out. Sometimes the first step can be as simple as permitting yourself to be protected. Once you do this, you can start walking toward standing fully in your power and Medicine. This helps to stabilize your energy field and takes practice and continuous self-reflection. It's a lifelong journey.

Medicine Reflection: Where in your life do you feel you need protection? Place your hands on your body where you feel the most vulnerable and tell yourself that you are worthy of guardianship. If you need extra support, you can always call on the fierceness of Wolf.

CAPACITY

One of the biggest things I have taken away from my somatic processing work has been the importance of assessing our capacity at any given moment. While this seems like a simple thing to do, I have never seen this encouraged or supported in our modern life. Capitalism and patriarchal structures tell us that we need to be "on" at all times. There's no time to rest or even to take a moment to assess whether or not we can agree to something. This causes us to bypass what our body, heart, and Spirit are feeling. We say yes to everything without actually asking ourselves if we have the emotional, physical, or spiritual energy to engage in what is asked of us. If we permit ourselves to take a moment of presence, we can assess how much energy we have to hold space or offer Medicine. It is such a gift to ask myself every day: "What is my capacity?"

There are things that I show up for because I have to, like making my children meals or putting them to bed, but I still acknowledge that sometimes my capacity is very low in those moments. By not bypassing those feelings, I am honoring my system and will choose rest more often when I need it. I get many requests for podcasts, workshops, and other events, and now I run each of those through my "capacity meter." There are times when it can be challenging to assess what my capacity might be if the event is a few weeks or months away, but I have learned that my body always knows. My capacity meter always shows up in my lymph nodes and my chest. I will feel pangs in these areas if I push past my capacity or say yes to too many things. I have learned to listen carefully to my body and know that it holds deep wisdom.

Maybe your awareness of your capacity shows up as a mental or emotional knowing, for example:

- Your brain feels full, foggy, or overwhelmed.

- Your schedule has so many appointments on it you cannot fit in one more thing.

- You are forgetful.

- You get angry, resentful, or teary when asked to give something.

- You find yourself snappy or irritable over seemingly small things.

Only you know how much energy you have to expend at any given moment. Your energy is your own.

Medicine Reflection: Take a moment to find your own "capacity meter." On a scale of 1 to 10, how full is your bucket? What is your capacity in this moment?

Your Sacred No

I want to be clear in this conversation surrounding your sacred right to say no and set boundaries, that if you walk with pain and trauma around your body sovereignty and agency not being respected or honored, I see you. If you have a story of physical, emotional, or spiritual abuse where your "no's" weren't heard, seen, or acknowledged, I'm so sorry this has been part of your path. It is not okay in any way that someone caused you to experience this, and it is not your fault. If you didn't receive the protection that is your divine birthright as a child or young person from those who were meant to guard you, I offer deep compassion. While many of us carry lived experience around our sacred boundaries not being honored, we may also carry Ancestral trauma from our parents or generations before us who also experienced this. This is big work, and if you have chosen to do it, I am so proud of you. It takes immense courage.

How many times has a yes come out of your mouth when your body and Spirit were whispering no? Or maybe it wasn't a whisper, but a scream, and you still couldn't bring yourself to form the word no. As a recovering people-pleaser, this has been a growth edge, and I have learned that saying no is profoundly sacred.

Saying no offers:

- more potency and meaning to my yes.
- deep healing to all of the parts of myself that I am not willing to abandon.

- stability to my energetic field and boundaries.
- space for the other person to step into their own capabilities.

I started my business before social media appeared in our world, but when I moved my Medicine there, I started to receive private messages daily: "What homeopathic remedy do I need for this sore toe?" "I had a dream last night about a fox; what does that mean?" "What's the name of my Spirit Guide?" and so on. I felt frustrated and resentful, wondering why people thought they had unlimited access to my energy and Medicine without any offer of exchange. I would march around my house muttering, "How do they not know how much time and energy this takes me?" or "Why don't they honor my Medicine?" After months of throwing daily pity parties, I realized that it was up to me to show people where my boundaries were. It was up to me to speak to what was and wasn't okay. You may have heard before that you need to "teach and show people how you want to be treated." Speaking up for myself and framing my no with a boundary was one of the ways I did this.

I set up a structure for questions such as this where the person could book a 15-minute time slot, pay for my time and energy, and then we could jump on a call or converse over email. The fascinating thing was when I set this up, the requests began to disappear. The simple act of me setting this boundary, as Wolf does brilliantly, and asking for the reciprocity that I desired shifted the energy almost immediately. My time, energy, and Medicine are sacred. And so are yours. When we say no, we are actually making room for more aligned opportunities to come our way. A question that I love to ask myself is: *If I say no to this, what am I saying yes to?*

Being in tune with your body sensations, emotions, and thoughts when a request comes your way can take practice. Again, if you carry a history of abuse in your body or even in your lineage, this can be a really challenging journey. You are worthy of support and help to move through all of this pain. It is valid, and you are not to blame. Healing in safe and brave spaces is possible. You are so worthy of receiving this.

Wolf Medicine Invocation

Dearest Wolf, thank you for reminding me that I am precious and worthy of saying no. I am grateful for your ability to track the energies that are not supportive or aligned for my Spirit or body. I promise to listen more deeply to the subtle signs and signals that something is awry. When needed, I welcome in your growl and honor your ability to see when my energy is being invaded or impacted by others. Thank you for assisting me with walking in potent protection; I am grateful for your fierce guardianship.

Mshkawji Giizis Moon Affirmation

As the Star Nations lower to meet me, I am protected and surrounded in Cosmic energy. I am worthy, standing in my fierce power, and I let the world around me see the flames of my brilliance. My energy is precious and deserves guarding when needed. I am the Medicine.

CHAPTER 13

MNIDOONS GIIZISOONHG LITTLE SPIRIT MOON

Our twelfth Moon of Creation that happens in November is a time where we dream good health into being. As we walk toward healing, we remember that we are already whole. This Moon teaches us that when we focus our intentions on our healing, we gain deep wisdom. During this time, our inner Healers are activated, and we pay attention to how to listen more deeply to their voice and presence. This Moon reminds us that we are all on a healing path, and we can choose to cultivate deep wisdom from the struggles and challenges that we may walk through. We can be the Healers of our own lives, and this Moon calls us to share what we have learned for the good of our communities, our families, and our soul purpose.

MOON LEGEND: HOW THE LITTLE SPIRIT CAME TO BE

The humans were the last part of the vision that Creator had for the inhabitants of the Earthly plane. When humans were dreamed into being, Creator left room for evolution and planted this capacity in their DNA. For hundreds of years, humans walked around the Earth in deep relationship with their physical body. They focused on how strong their bodies were as they hunted, gathered, and fought for survival. Humans mastered their relationship with their physical body and grew to carry themselves with great vigor. As Creator watched this growth, they knew that there was another aspect to what could make humans whole. They infused a brilliant light into their hearts, which taught humans how to feel. Love, grief, anger, compassion, rage, and shame began to move through the humans, and they practiced learning how to relate to one another through these emotions.

Sadly, the humans seemed to struggle to come back to love and compassion in their interactions, and disagreements became daily occurrences. Humans harmed and wounded one another. Creator was very sad, for this wasn't their intended vision. They saw the humans becoming rigid and mean and watched them abuse and offend one another. Creator knew they must do something to create mending and repair. They saw that the humans needed another aspect to their beings, one that would support their evolution and growth. They called it the Spirit.

Creator infused divine energy into each human being, weaving this Spirit through every layer and level of the body, mind, and emotions. The humans breathed sighs of relief when this was offered, for they had felt devoid of this light. As they were activated with Spirit, they stared at one another in awe. Never had they seen so much beauty in one another, never had they felt so connected.

To protect this aspect of divinity, Creator blew one final piece into each human. They called it the Little Spirit, an inherent vital force that pulsed through the human experience. It was profoundly precious and informed each person's well-being. Creator explained that the Little Spirit needed tending and protection, for it was delicate at times. The Little Spirit could be knocked out of the human as a result of unkind words or abusive treatment. It could be impacted by any traumatic event, so it needed to be cared for.

This Little Spirit was planted in each person with the intention that it would help them focus on their innate ability to heal themselves. If the Little Spirit was harmed in any way, the human would know, and there would be a signal that it was time to focus on healing. All humans needed to do was listen deeply and hear the call so homeostasis could return. It was a vital part of the human experience, and with its introduction, Creator saw love and compassion return. From that day forward, humans continued to evolve, with the Spirit being an essential part of their Medicine walk. They learned that all healing was possible, and when things were out of alignment, they could call on this profound vital force to remember that they were already whole.

Animal Spirit: *Ginebig* (Snake)

The Animal Spirit that best represents our twelfth Moon of Creation is Snake, or as they are known in Anishiinabemowin, *Ginebig.* Snake Medicine speaks to the transformative process of healing our bodies, minds, and Spirits. Snake shows up to remind us that we all carry innate healing abilities and helps us to acknowledge and fine-tune this gift. Snake's belly is rooted to the Earth Mother and, therefore, helps amplify our sacred connection. There is deep wisdom, life force, and support available to us from Mother Earth, and we are asked to walk gently and graciously. With healing, we shed layers of the past, just like Snake sheds their skin. As the layers fall to the Earth, they are mulched and transmuted into supportive Medicine that holds us. Snake reminds us of the power of staying grounded in life to bring our physical, emotional, and spiritual energies into balance.

Snake Message

- You are a Healer.
- The Earth provides grounding Medicine.
- It's time to shed the past.
- All healing is possible.

You Are Not Broken

For many years, immersed in the world of alternative healing, I was bombarded with the message that my body was broken. You would think that the messages I received walking this nontraditional path would have been positive and nourishing to my Spirit, but most were not. In my early 20s, naturopaths consistently told me that I had to detox, cleanse, and restrict; that I needed to purge the toxins and sickness from my body. They listened to my symptoms and story, and instead of asking more questions, they would list all the things that were wrong with me. As I searched for healing, I heard the same negative messages repeatedly from a variety of practitioners; it wasn't just naturopaths who worked in this way. I tried everything, including juices, cleanses, vegan diets, supplements, fasts, and more. Most of what was offered up as a solution was not sustainable over the long term, nor was it rooted in love or self-compassion. This is not to say that I didn't receive support or aspects of healing during these times, but the experiences simply did not meet me in the fullness of where I needed to be met. I wasn't healing.

Looking back, I am blown away by the fact that no one thought to ask me about the Ancestral wounds that I had been holding in my cells, DNA, and blood. No one looked at the impact of the intergenerational trauma of colonization, oppression, and attempted genocide I carried in my body. The modalities were touted as holistic, yet there were important pieces left out of the conversation. Many of these practitioners said that they were also operating from a holistic approach, yet they were consistently missing the mark by failing to address the impacts of systemic and cultural effects on health and wellness. We are not broken; our systems are. The lack of acknowledgment of these issues saddens me, but my experiences as I've searched for answers have also been gifts—because they've pushed me to dig deeper to find the root of my sickness in generational trauma. As I unraveled and healed through all that I had supressed, I learned how I could effectively help others dig deep, heal, and be seen in their fullest expression.

The day that homeopathy was introduced to me was a day I will never forget. My practitioner offered me two tiny pellets, a homeopathic remedy called Silicea, for my "sensitivity as a child." At the time, I was seeing her for all of these physical symptoms and wondered why my emotional state as a child mattered. How could this homeopathic remedy change the physical symptoms I was experiencing? In a matter of weeks my fear of death, hair loss, skin eruptions, and joint pain were noticeably better. I felt more connected and remembered aspects of myself that had felt buried. The remedy addressed both my physical and emotional pain, even old trauma. I felt held in my wholeness with my practitioner holding love for both my shadow parts and my light. I knew that if homeopathy could provide that for me, that it could do this for others. I set off on a journey to learn this Medicine to help others see that healing is possible. I've used homeopathy for healing for over 20 years, and I can genuinely say that it has unearthed deep Ancestral trauma and pain from my soul and brought me into a space of hope and thriving.

Learning about homeopathy opened my eyes to other forms of energy Medicine, and I began to see different avenues that could support my healthy smoothies-and-vitamins regimen. I learned that the most important thing about any approach to wellness is that we are seen as whole, never broken. As mentioned in chapter 4, in reference to Deer Medicine, shame can be a barrier to deep healing. Messages of inadequacy around our bodies, minds, and souls have a great impact. I wonder what would be possible if we were held, seen, and supported through the lens of unconditional love. What would be possible if when we sat before someone, they saw us as the exquisite beings that we are, in their highest form of expression—just as the first humans did after they received their piece of Little Spirit. So much healing is possible from this space. It's miraculous. I've seen it.

As I continued to practice, I realized that just like a homeopathic remedy, my presence and space holding could act as a catalyst for or reminder of someone's innate healing force. Each person who came to me was already whole—they carried all the potential needed within them for healing—they had just lost sight of the aspects connecting them to that power. Little Spirit Moon reminds us to reconnect to the power of our wholeness, to remember we are much more than our symptoms and disease labels.

> **Medicine Reflection:** In what ways have different systems told you that you are broken? Do you believe that you have the ability to heal yourself? Why or why not?

YOUR INNER HEALER

Your Inner Healer is powerful. Throughout this book, we have moved through exercises, journeys, and rituals to remind us of the capacity we all have to heal ourselves. We are all Healers. It's something I have shared with my children time and time again when they have a cut, a bruise, or a simple cold. Your body and Spirit know what to do. They always carry an incredible vital force that moves toward healing. Sometimes we just have to release the blocks gently. This vital healing force has shown up many times in my own life and those of my patients. In our Indigenous understanding, we recognize our Inner Healer as the "Little Spirit," that pulse of Creation that moves through us. When there is trauma, the delicate Little Spirit cannot thrive. But we can bring healing and balance back through different modalities, both physical and energetic. Homeopathy and energy work are both beautiful ways to support our Little Spirit.

Through my lens, I know that healing is possible, and there is always hope. I also know how complex and nuanced healing can be. There are many moments in my life that stand out to me as evidence of my Inner Healer at work, but I want to preface this by sharing my experience through a body that lives with a chronic illness impacted by generational trauma. Colonization has tried to break my connection with my Inner Healer, and I believe that our current systems try to do this to all of us. It has been a journey of holding it all with compassion and refusing to bypass lived experience. If you feel frustrated by the advice that all you need to do is speak positive affirmations and envision good health, I see you. This is deep work for many. There can be a different way. I've experienced it, and so have many of those whom I have served with my Medicine.

The day I was diagnosed with lupus, something came alive in my soul. I felt on a mission to heal myself and knew that the answers had to be somewhere. We are conditioned to believe that the answers are outside us, and I truly looked everywhere for them before I looked inward. I have tried it all. I went to Peru to the highest navigable lake in the world to sit in ritual, and experienced Shake Tent Ceremonies, watching miracles happen before my eyes. I have been gifted sacred tools and been told I am a Pipe carrier. I have done colonics, raw food diets, soul retrievals, somatic therapy, Plant Medicines, breath work, and so much more. I have studied and participated in hundreds of courses, sessions, and Ceremonies, just to learn that it all comes back to me. While I trust that doctors, Healers, psychics, specialists, et cetera, can help direct or facilitate healing, the most potent Guide is you. The more we can build relationship with our inner wise one, the more we can build the capacity to trust that we have way more sovereignty than we thought we did. We truly are the Medicine.

These experiences have nourished me and supported me in many ways, and I am deeply grateful for all that I have learned. With every aspect of support, my Inner Healer is nourished. I have learned that I can ask for and receive brilliant support on my path, but ultimately, I am responsible for how this healing touches me. The more I work on receiving and feeling worthy of wellness and health, the more my Inner Healer is fed.

I have so much compassion for those who have had heartbreaking experiences in their journey toward motherhood.

If this is your experience, I hold you in love. When I wanted to have children, the expert doctors said this to me: "With the specific lupus antibodies that you carry, I would highly suggest you don't try. You are guaranteed to lose your baby. If I were a traffic light, I would give you the red light." I remember leaving the hospital that day, clearing his words out of my ears and heart. I smudged when I got home and put some Tobacco down on the Earth. "Creator, if I am meant to have this baby, please show me a sign." I know that some would call this irresponsible, but I knew deep in my bones that a soul was meant to come to this Earth through me.

Shortly after this experience, I remember having a dream of holding a baby in my arms. It was so clear that I knew it was a possibility, so I took the words the doctor said, filtered it through my knowing, and tried to conceive. When my first son was two, I asked him how he knew that I was meant to be his mama. He told me that he looked down from the Stars, saw me, and then pressed a button. Something in his soul knew that my womb space was meant to be part of his Creation story. It felt miraculous that after years of hearing doctors say I couldn't have a child, I did. Twice.

There have been times when my lupus symptoms have been so severe that I have been unable to walk or put my socks on, times when I could barely take a step up the stairs, write, or play the piano. During those moments, I felt helpless, and as though nothing would ever get better, so I understand why it's so easy to lose hope and feel like our bodies are betraying us. Every time I listened to what my body needed, through rest, healing work, or even pharmaceuticals, I was able to come back into balance. Am I cured? No. Have I healed? Yes, so many times. This is how I know, deep in my bones, that healing can happen. It might not always look the way we want it to look, but it's available to us through our connection with our Inner Healer.

MEDICINE JOURNEY
Find Your Inner Healer

Find a comfortable space to sit or lie down and welcome in Snake Spirit. Pay attention to your breath. See yourself walking through a golden door that is holding space for your transformation. Snake appears on the Earth at your feet, and you feel deeply rooted to the Land. Follow Snake as they lead you to a path that leads down to a body of Water that is familiar to you; it's beautiful and nourishing. Snake asks you to get down to the Earth, placing your belly against the Land. Feel the unconditional love of the Earth Mother flowing through you, rooting you and grounding you. Snake offers you their Medicine as you do this, reminding you that life is a journey of evolution, growth, and remembering. Any layers that need to be shed are released here.

Stand back up and dip your toes into the Water's edge. Feel the Water begin to wash over your feet gently, and walk in as deep as you feel comfortable going. The Water is illuminated with the energy of the light streaming down from the Sun. As it dances across the body of Water, the light begins to remind your vital force of its power and potential. It reminds you that you can heal yourself. Appearing before you, gently skimming the top of the Water, is your Inner Healer. They are radiating vitality and life force. Take a moment to observe them and ask yourself:

- How do they appear?
- What are they wearing?
- What are they here to help you heal today?
- What guidance do they have to share?

As they stand before you, an incredible rush of energy radiates from them to you, holding a certain vibration and color. This color is your Spirit Color; see it wrapping around you, informing deeper healing for your system. You now carry this color radiance from head to toe, and it wraps around you, becoming a cape. You may want to wear this color when you feel you need healing or deeper connection.

Your Inner Healer comes close and opens their arms to you. If it resonates for you to step forward to align with them, do so now. Breathe deeply as they infuse your cells, organs, and tissues with the highest healing vibrations. All the spaces in between vibrate with wellness, light, and health. Remember that you have always carried this ability within and you have now amplified it. Snake tells you that it's time to go, and you follow them back to the path and back to the door where you started. Take one last breath into your belly and feel your Inner Healer now ignited. Your Little Spirit and vital force pulse powerfully. *You are the Medicine.*

Medicine Reflection: Where do you feel your Inner Healer in your body? What are they sharing with you?

SACRED WATERS

There was a teacher I worked with named Cindy who facilitated a lot of womb healing, and she shared about the importance of nurturing and paying attention to our Sacred Waters. She reminded me that everything we expose ourselves to energetically and physically has an impact on our Waters. This made sense to me as a homeopath, as I knew that Water carried both memory and cultural significance, as Water is our first Medicine. Indigenous women are the Water protectors; Water affects and connects us all. In our Water Ceremonies, we use copper cups and buckets to gather and pray over the Water, the copper acting as a conductor for our energy. We guard the Water fiercely for all of Creation. It is crucial to protect the Earth's Waters, and we are Earth, so we must nurture our inner Waters, too. We are made up of approximately 60 percent Water, the beautiful vibration listening, flowing, waiting for healing transmission.

I like to ask myself and those I offer healing to the following questions. Take a moment to answer them as honestly as you can:

- What words do you speak to your Sacred Waters?

- What are the energies you expose them to? (Some examples are television, movies, social media, and relational energies.)

- How do you nourish your Sacred Waters? What are they calling for today?

- What intentions and vibrations do you want to infuse into your Sacred Waters in this moment?

Activate your Inner Healer and place those intentions in all the liquids you drink, the Water you bathe in, and the Water you use. Always start with gratitude, for we are so blessed to have clean Water; it is a true privilege that many of my people and others don't have.

TEARS ARE SACRED

People have told me stories filled with grief, trauma, and heartache as I sat with them in their healing. Tears sprang to my eyes often as I felt the depth of their pain. In homeopathy school, we were taught to keep a neutral face, and after 15 years, I have finally come to terms with the fact that I can't always do this. Usually, I would spend some time trying to gently blow air up to my eyes to dry the puddles beginning to form there. I always kept those interactions "professional," and my clients probably never noticed. But after all those years, I realized that living through our human experience is a vulnerable act of courage, and tears are sacred, a flowing aspect of our Sacred Waters. An Elder taught me the Ancestral wisdom and Medicine that tears hold. Since we know that Water holds incredible vibration, take a moment to think about the impact that spilling your Sacred Waters into the world might have. We work so hard to suppress them, yet they are Medicine waiting to be shared.

> **Medicine Reflection:** When is the last time you cried? Are there any tears currently suppressed in your heart, throat, or soul? What wisdom might they hold?

GROUNDING

If you have been in the New Age or spiritual spaces, you will have heard of the importance of "grounding" ourselves and feeling comfortable to be fully present in our physical bodies. For many folks, especially for those who have experienced trauma or illness, our bodies have not always felt safe and comfortable. This trauma could also extend to intergenerational trauma and past lives. In the past few years, I have learned from some amazing somatic therapy teachers, and slowly, my body has felt like a safe place to be. For a very long time, when I encountered a situation that my system registered as dangerous based on my past trauma, I could feel my Spirit leave my body. I attracted many clients who have had this experience—being out of our bodies is sometimes easier for those of us who found this Earthly plane too dense. In my practice, I found a mix of trauma and heightened sensitivity to be a recipe for us living outside of our bodies. My therapist recently shared this wisdom with me: "disassociation is intelligence too."

Being grounded in our bodies allows our vital force to take up more space and create health and well-being. When we are aligned and rooted in our physical bodies, healing energy can then touch all the parts that were previously shut away from it. Trauma or disconnect creates bubbles around areas of our body so our vital force cannot reach them. Those areas become frozen, blocked off from the flow. When we begin to thaw and come back to the presence in our body, there is capacity for more flow, abundance, health, and light.

While our bodies may not always feel safe, Mother Earth has always been beneath us, holding us steady. You will find me walking barefoot or wearing my buckskin moccasins, practices that help me to remember the Earth is holding me and it's safe to walk embodied. The sound of the drum is another Medicine tool that allows us to feel grounded. The drumbeat represents the first heartbeat we ever heard, our Mother's. When we listen to it, this sound connects to that feeling of being surrounded in safety and love. Furthermore, we can place our hands on our heart at any time to feel our inner drumbeat. Whenever I attend a pow wow where the big drums are being played, I instantly tear up with that feeling of remembering. It's powerful Medicine and helps me to stay rooted in my body.

The most essential step in grounding, however, is to first create that safety in your body. This could be done through somatic/embodied practices such as shaking, soothing, tapping, drumming, dancing. If you are interested in this work,

I highly recommend finding a somatic therapy practitioner. I have discovered somatic work to be one of the most effective ways of building safety in one's body. Once you feel safe to be embodied, the other ways of grounding are much more effective.

When you are ready, there are many different ways to practice grounding into your body, and they are all helpful. Here are a few practices:

- Envision yourself as a tree with roots that extend from the base of your spine and move them into the Earth. Stand tall and feel the pulse of the Earth moving through your roots. Breathe that energy up into your body.

- Ask for Snake Medicine to show you the way. Practice lying on the Earth, belly to her Soil. Draw in her Medicine.

- Listen to drumming or practice drumming yourself. Let the vibrations of the drum call you into your body.

- Stand barefoot on the Land and feel Mother Earth's heartbeat pulsing through your feet.

- Place your hands on your heart and feel your inner drumbeat; let it remind you of the first heartbeat you ever heard and all of the hearts that support you.

A powerful practice to realign with the first drumbeat we heard is to journey back to our Mother's Womb space. I have facilitated this journey for many, and it is a beautiful practice to bring back the remembering of our connection to our first Water experience. There is often much healing that is needed here, for every one of us marinated in all that our mothers felt and experienced during that sacred time—the good and the bad. If you were born into a body with ovaries and a uterus, you may have heard that you were born with all of the eggs you will ever have in your lifetime. Therefore, when your Mother was developing in your Grandmother's womb, you existed as an egg in your Mother's ovaries. Your Grandmother carried a part of you within her, literally. Bringing awareness to healing through our maternal lineage has a whole new meaning when we realize this. Our healing ripples generations back and infuses into the generations to come. When we are aligned with our Inner Healer, we can see just how powerful we are.

Snake Medicine Invocation

Dearest Snake, thank you for reminding me that I have powerful healing abilities within. I am grateful for your reminder that I can shed all the layers of myself that are no longer serving me. Help me to speak kindly to my Sacred Waters and remember to be conscious of who and what I expose them to. Remind me of the Earth's grounding and stable Medicine, as I walk embodied. I promise to continue building a relationship with my Inner Healer, acknowledging the power I hold as I receive guidance and facilitation from others. I am grateful for your reminders that I am already whole, and that wellness is my divine birthright.

Mnidoons Giizisoonhg Moon Affirmation

I remember the beauty of my Little Spirit, and I hold them with tenderness and reverence. I ask this Moon to wash my Sacred Waters with light and love. Healing is available to me always. I am the Medicine.

○ ꒰ ꒰ ꒰ ꒱ ꒱ ● ꒰ ꒰ ꒰ ꒰ ◯

CHAPTER 14

MNIDOONS GIIZIS
BIG SPIRIT MOON

Our thirteenth Moon of Creation is in December, when we reflect on the Medicine journey that we have taken over the past year. We have been moving closer to darkness, and on the day of the Winter Solstice, the light begins to return. We are reminded of how bright we shine during this time, even amid the shadows we carry. Without the dark, we would not see the Moon and the Stars. This Moon pulls on our Sacred Waters for us to expand and shine as brilliantly as Creator dreamed for us. We are meant to stand tall as we dream our visions into being. We weave our healing into the world because we are born for this. We are the Medicine Keepers.

Moon Legend: How the Dreamcatcher Came to Be

A *Nokomis* (Grandmother) was sitting on her rocking chair, knitting some clothing for her grandchildren. Her grandson was playing on the floor at her feet. Suddenly, Spider scurried across the floor, and the child stood up to chase and kill it. *"Gibichiwebinan!"* (Stop it!), she said. "Spider is our relative, and we need to tend to them as such. They are our Kin. Every part of Creation depends on another. Please don't kill other living beings." The boy looked surprised and then apologized to his *Nokomis*. "I'm sorry, Grandmother. I didn't know. From now on, I will see that all beings are worthy of life. I will be more careful."

The Grandmother told the boy to play outside, and she continued rocking in her chair and knitting. A little while later, Spider approached *Nokomis* and offered gratitude. *"Miigwetch*, thank you for saving my life. My heart is so grateful and I want to create some Medicine for you." Spider began to weave something beautiful into being and when it was complete, they offered it to the Grandmother. "This is called a Dreamcatcher," Spider said. "Its Medicine is potent and powerful for your people. When you hang it over your bed, it protects your Dreamtime. Any bad dreams get caught in the web, healed, and transmuted. The good dreams pass right through. This will be good Medicine for all who use it with gratitude and reverence."

Nokomis thanked Spider for this gift and hung it over the little boy's bed to remind him that there is Medicine held by every Animal and every aspect of Creation. The Dreamcatcher has provided Medicine to our people ever since and reminds us that we are constantly dreaming our world into being. Grandmother Spider is the gatekeeper of this Medicine, holding space for the enormous potential of our lives.

This story has been passed down to me through my communication with Elders.

Animal Spirit: *Asabikeshiinh* (Spider)

The Animal Spirit that best represents our thirteenth Moon of Creation is Spider, or as they are known in Anishinabemowin, *Asabikeshiinh*. Spider Medicine speaks to how we weave our destiny. We are creators, infusing our intentions into intricate and beautiful manifestations. Spider teaches us to be patient and trust what we are building. With time and dedication, we will receive what we desire. This Medicine reminds us that our creations are filled with the strength distilled from our past experiences, and that our web of Creation is resilient. Magic is an everyday occurrence and meets us when we open our eyes to see. We are dream weavers, and Spider assists us to masterfully move toward our desires with tenacity, reverence, and practice.

Spider Message

- You are a sacred part of the web of Creation.
- You can weave your dreams into being.
- Your web is filled with remembering, reclaiming, and rising.
- Beauty is waiting.

LIVING IN THE DREAM

You may have heard the phrase "dreaming our life into being" used by folks who practice shamanism or Indigenous healing ways. Dr. Alberto Villoldo has taught about how "the Shaman lives in the dream," and how "the task is to dream with our eyes open—to envision the possible before they envision the probable." We all can direct and guide this dream. When I first heard the phrase "dreaming our life into being," I realized that my system already knew how to do this and that I had lived lifetimes in this knowing. I thought back to when I was a little girl and would tell my mother about "what I had imagined" the night before. I thought about how dreams informed my Medicine walk and how we continuously work with the luminous strands of the spiritual and energetic realms. My web appears as a beautiful matrix of energy, much like a luminous Dreamcatcher, each strand held by the Grandmothers who channel through me and my Ancestors and Guides who support me. When we can access the energetic realms, so much becomes possible. I have dreamed my children, my private practice, my global Medicine circle, this book, an oracle deck, and so much more into being. I have dreamed of sacred friendships, trips to the ocean, magical synchronicities, and love. Some may call it miraculous, others manifestation. I love to have my eyes wide open, tapping into the energetic matrix of possibility and reweaving what is calling for my attention.

We dream our Medicine into being every day through our lived experiences, our choice to bring healing to our struggles, and our openness to share wisdom with others. To stay rooted in your dream, you must hold on to your vision. I see our vision as a living, breathing energy that flows through our energetic web. We must tend to it daily with inspired action so that our dreams come alive.

Medicine Reflection: What are you dreaming into being?

MEDICINE EXPRESSION

In this book, I have shared how I came to illuminate my Medicine in the world. Spirit moved me, and Creator had a vision for how I would spread my wings. Every step of the way, I learned about all the tools shared in this book. This is how I know that doing your inner work and consciously responding to what calls for healing in your life can become the wisdom you share with others. This wisdom, combined with the gifts you came here with naturally, can be life changing. Your Medicines are the result of your unique path through life, and I am here celebrating that uniqueness with every cell of my being. What I know to be true is that we need you fully expressed. Listen to the call of your soul, to your reason for being. Your Ancestors dreamed you here, so, as Mary Oliver famously wrote: "Tell me, what is it you plan to do with your one wild and precious life?"

One of the misconceptions that we hold is that we somehow need to be perfectly healed before putting our Medicine out in the world. I have heard many say, "How can I help others heal when I still struggle?" Here is the truth: we are all going to continue to move through cycles of darkness and light until we die. This is how we evolve. If we were completely "healed," we probably wouldn't need to be here any longer and would leave the Earthly plane. Let us normalize the imperfect human experience. Those whom you look up to and place on pedestals? They fall. Those whom you think have it all together? They don't. We are all in this messy life together, walking each other back home to the Cosmos. You have what you need, right here, right now, to spread your wings and rise. It's written in the Stars.

Another barrier that keeps us stuck in the same patterns is thinking that we need just one more course, certification, or acronym after our name to have the qualifications we need to serve in our Medicine. I am all for taking classes, learning, working with mentors and teachers, but if this is all you are doing, without any action or practice, you are missing out on a considerable part of your Medicine Walk. Studying can be an essential step toward mastery, but when we pivot to action, this is where our dreams start gaining traction. We need to practice.

> **Medicine Reflection:** Think about all the courses, degrees, workshops, books, life experiences, past-life experiences, et cetera, from which you have gained wisdom and experienced growth. Write this list on a piece of paper and see how much you have to offer the world.

REFRAMING FAILURE

Folks often ask me how I can intuit things so quickly or see visions with ease. Even though this was a gift I have carried my whole life, it took practice to refine it and I have practiced with thousands of people. In my homeopathic practice I didn't always choose the most beneficial remedies for my patients, and I learned from every mistake that I made. The most profound learning comes when I walk with a growth mind-set. Practice is my path to mastery, challenges are welcomed as part of the process, failures don't mean anything about my inherent worth, and everything that comes my way is an opportunity for growth.

We learn so much from making mistakes, from getting up and trying again. Before every single circle, workshop, or speaking engagement, I feel nervous. "What if I fail? What if they don't like what I say? What if I fumble my words or forget something?" I have doubted myself, questioned my skills, and worried that I wasn't quite ready to do whatever

I had scheduled to do. I have walked out of my events wondering if people had a good time or got anything out of it, worried that I wasn't enough to heal anyone. Every experience of doubt and wondering helped me to grow. Every mistake helped me to do better the next time. There are people who might find some version of success overnight, but this is rare. If you had peered into my heart over the past two decades, you would have seen a lot of tears and doubts about whether or not to continue. You would have seen many course corrections after feeling like I had failed miserably. After over two decades of facilitating healing work, I have grown in confidence, determination, and certainty. I know that "failure" means nothing about who I am at my core. Just like Spider Medicine teaches, I am a divine part of the Creation web, no matter what, and so are you. It takes courage to put your Medicines out in the world, and our world needs our healing essence now more than ever before. Be courageous enough to do things imperfectly. With practice, dedication, and commitment, we move toward mastery.

Over the years of dreaming my purpose into being, the two things that have helped me to rise are: frequently stretching my soul out of its comfort zone and a deep commitment to my inner landscape. As I put my Medicine out into the world, I had to stretch out of my comfort zone. At the beginning of my journey, this consisted of joining networking groups and teaching to small groups. I eventually shifted to being visible on social media, creating larger communities, and agreeing to more significant speaking engagements. During every step on this path, I have been nervous and wondered if I was enough. Every time I said yes to something that felt out of my comfort zone, I was worried that I couldn't do it somehow. But I would remember my Ancestors behind me and the call of my soul. I would remember how far I've come and all the things I've transmuted in my life.

I would remember the things people would say about how I've impacted them and how my presence has changed their lives. And this propelled me forward. Moving beyond your comfort zone is a challenge, but you can't turn back if there is a fire in your belly. When it's your time, it's your time.

Every day I see everything that comes my way as a healing opportunity, and I meet each one with a dedicated heart. The most significant leaps of my life come from self-reflection and inner work with energy Medicine and other forms of healing. My inner landscape informs the outer landscape that surrounds me. Bringing my shadows to the light is the most profound way that things shift in my life. Every aspect of myself that I pour healing energy into offers me a ten-fold return on investment. A Medicine Person once told me, "You can only go as deep with others as you choose to go yourself." This helped me to see that I would be a better space holder and facilitator of healing if I committed to this path of inner healing personally. When I unweave a part of my story that isn't serving me anymore, I can tap more authentically into the incredible matrix of energy all around me. My capacity to receive beauty, peace, abundance, and joy expands as I dive deep.

> **Medicine Reflection:** What is the next leap or soul stretch that is calling you? What thoughts arise as you feel into it?

IMPACT

Whenever I am doubting my path or wondering if I am making a difference, I ask myself what kind of impact I want to make and then take intentional action. As I mentioned in chapter 10, every so often, I will get a message from someone saying, "You may not remember me, but I saw you many years ago and you changed my life." These messages will often shock me as I think back to those moments, and I don't remember doing anything superhuman or particularly remarkable. I just showed up as myself. I held space. I stood in my Medicine, and I loved people up.

My dreams for the long-term impact of my work include:

- I want people to know that they carry a brilliant, energetic presence and purpose.

- I want people to remember the healing power they carry.

- I want people to reclaim the parts of themselves that have been forgotten or oppressed by the systems at play.

- I want people to have many glimpses of their divine nature and see that they are a part of this magical tapestry we call life.

We all have the potential to plant seeds and inspire others. Sometimes that impact isn't always seen right away. This can be challenging in a world that leans toward instant gratification, so we must trust that as we take steps toward our dreams, that the waves of impact are happening. If you identify as a Healer or work in the energetic realms, sometimes this can be even more challenging, as much of our work is intangible. I want to remind you that this work is compelling and potent.

Doing the behind-the-scenes work, the inner work, the work in the spiritual and energetic realms, the work in our dreams and visions . . . Parenting your children in a new way, breaking cycles, trailblazing paths that are not yet formed . . . If you can relate to showing up in any of these ways in the world, please know that you are seen and valued. Our capitalistic and patriarchal measurements of what "good work" is can take us off track. Sometimes the progress we make in the unseen and invisible realms is what moves the needle forward. I always love to remind myself that while the world may not witness my progress and growth through a viral Instagram post, my Ancestors are always witnessing. And that, my friends, is enough.

LET MAGIC MOVE YOU

When we live knowing that there is an energetic matrix of support for our dreams and co-create it, we build more capacity for magic. A few years back, I was drawn to take a course with Susanna Maida about how to do Medicine Walks. I was pregnant at the time and experiencing a lot of fear around the upcoming birth, but I figured I was signing up for a straightforward class to learn about a new Ceremony that I could use to support my clients. Nothing life-altering there. One day we were asked to take a walk on the Land and notice how it might be helping our healing process. I saw a sign on my walk that said, "You are not broken." Because I had broken my pelvis during my first birth experience, these words initiated a river of tears. I remember feeling a rush of healing energy from the Land. It held me, and I released grief that I had held for four years. I was not expecting this emotional outpouring. I thought the course would teach me skills for my students, but instead the energy of that circle helped to heal something deep inside of me.

That day, I learned about getting out of my head and trusting my body and Spirit. Magic moved through me when I said yes to taking this training and guided me to that sign. It wasn't what I expected; it was way more potent. We don't always know what the outcome might be when we try something new. The healing energy alters us, moves us, and works us. Our minds cannot always make sense of it. Big Spirit Moon reminds us that magic moves us every day; all we need to do is acknowledge it and more comes our way. I have had many experiences where I have received direct transmission of the Medicine I needed, simply by being in the presence of a particular person and I take it as it comes. Whenever something happens that lights up my heart in magnificent ways, I look up to the Stars and say, "More of this, more of this." I am making magic my new normal.

> **Medicine Reflection:** What are the biggest moments of your life where magic moved you? Can you expand your capacity for more of these moments?

MAGNETIZE

We can intentionally become clear magnets for what we are dreaming of for our lives. Part of this practice involves moving through the healing journey that has been offered in this book. We build magnetic resilience every time we dive deep to do our healing work. We are more aligned and matched with our desired outcome with each healing breath and action. Our Medicine becomes magnetic as we clear out wounds, stories, and beliefs and stand in our sparkle. When we bring intention to our healing journey, we can then infuse our energy field with the Medicine our Ancestors dreamed for us. The sacred step of magnetizing involves integrating all that we have learned and weaving it into how we choose to show up every day. You might envision yourself as an actual magnet, a sparkling crystal, or a shining star; as you flow your essence out clearly, you reach those who are meant to be touched by your presence.

MEDICINE JOURNEY
Animal Activation

Envision that your energy field is now magnetic. Share these invocations aloud to call upon all of the Animal Medicines that have journeyed with us throughout this book to help you dream your visions into being. We call on Grandmother Spider to help us weave these intentions.

Turtle, remind me of my Creation story.

Thunderbird, illuminate my essence.

Bear, infuse me with the Great Mystery.

Deer, shower me with compassion.

Frog, purify and cleanse me.

Butterfly, transform my darkness into light.

Canada Goose, align me with community.

Porcupine, activate generational wisdom.

Crane, awaken my true path.

Eagle, help me to rise into my leadership.

Buffalo, infuse me with abundance.

Wolf, amplify and guard my sacred space.

Snake, deepen my connection with my Inner Healer.

Spider, weave my dreams into being.

You are a pulsing, brilliant, and magnetic force in the world. We call on your Ancestors to hold this field strong, and we call on your Spirit to integrate and shine in your magnificence. It's time to rise!

ACTIVATE YOUR SHINE

Shining our light takes a lot of courage, and it is the number one fear for those I mentor. Many of the folks I serve are highly sensitive, empathic beings, so they deeply feel everything. Some of the most common worries include:

- "If people knew the real me, they wouldn't like me."
- "I feel scared to take the first step."
- "What if my dreams never come true?"
- "What if I never find confidence?"
- "I can't shake that voice that tells me that I'm not good enough."

When we are making brave and bold moves in the world, not everyone will like us. We aren't for everyone, and that's okay. We need to focus on whom we are meant to impact. You may have heard: "Go where the love is!" As humans, we tend to fixate on the one person who criticizes us and not the hundreds who have been impacted by our Medicine Walk. The best advice I ever got was to walk a neutral path, not to attach myself to praise or criticism. Both have nothing to do with me.

I don't believe we will ever feel fully "ready" to share our gifts in bigger ways with the world. Through this book, I have offered practices that can build safety and heal though layers of what might be holding us back so that we are spreading our wings in ways that feel aligned. I believe that we can meet our fears and worries with compassion, reflection, and healing, and transform old beliefs that then propel us into action.

> **Medicine Reflection:** What holds you back from taking action toward your big dreams?

THE TRUTH ABOUT HUMILITY

As Anishinaabe people, we are asked to live by the Seven Grandfather Teachings: truth, love, bravery, respect, wisdom, honesty, and humility. Every day, in every interaction, I do my best to walk these in the world. The teaching of humility has always been one that I dance with, for to "be humble" has always held a connotation that invokes a feeling of smallness or shrinking. "Don't take up too much space! Don't brag about your accomplishments. If you radiate too brightly, people will think you are conceited." For me, this is not about humility, for the true meaning of humility in my heart is that we must stand as one with all of Creation. Just like the Big Spirit Moon shines in all her glory, we too have permission to shine in our fullness. Grandmother Spider reminds us that we are beautifully woven into the fabric of Creation, breathing the oxygen the Trees gift us, recycling the Waters of the Earth through our body, our cells fed and nourished by the Plants and Flowers. In this way, to walk with humility is to see our oneness with Creation as it reflects our beauty back to us. It's a teaching that asks us to walk side by side with the brilliance of the Sun, the rootedness of the tree trunks, and the softness of the snow. We are Earth, and humility asks us to stand tall and claim all that we are here to be. After all, you never see the Stars shrinking back, do you?

> **Medicine Reflection:** What does "be humble" mean to you? What aspect of Creation can you envision yourself as, as you embody true humility?

Become the Mentor You Needed

When I was first starting out in my work, I often wished for someone who understood some of the challenges I was facing in my life. Someone who had walked it a few steps ahead of me. On the days where I felt like I wasn't enough, I wanted to ask someone: "Do you feel this, too?" On the days where I wanted to give up because it felt lonely to walk as a Healer in this modern world, I wanted someone to tell me that I wasn't alone. These are the places where my Ancestors guided me, showed me, and illuminated my path. They told me to create what I've always needed and wanted. Install the guideposts for others to follow. Become the mentor and friend that I always wished was there to answer my questions. These are the places where my Ancestors guided me. It is here that my Mentorship weekends were birthed, along with my global online membership circle, and much more. I wanted to provide support for those who are seeking mentors. I wanted to create communities where we could see that we are never alone. Our desires are leading us to sacred creations. And if we can't find what we are searching for, perhaps it's time to blaze that trail and dream big dreams into being.

Medicine Reflection: What is the support you have craved in your life that you couldn't seem to find? How can you use this to direct your sacred Creations in the world?

MEDICINE JOURNEY
Upper World Retrieval

Find a comfortable space to sit or lie down and welcome in Spider Spirit. Grandmother Spider shows up and activates a Dreamcatcher around you. Through the spaces, you can see the darkness, for it is the time of the Winter Solstice. As you look up into the Sky, the Star Nations sparkle bright. The Upper Worlds are calling to you, and you feel yourself floating up toward the Stars. You leave your Dreamcatcher planted upon the Earth, for it is here to hold space for you to come back into your body when you return. As you soar, you feel your Spirit become free and light and you find yourself moving faster and faster. As you enter into the Cosmic frequency, you are flooded with light. You swoop and soar and float through the galaxies, the Stars and Planets remind you to take up the space you are here to take, and you see and feel the truth that you are made of Stardust. As you soar through the Stars, you see 14 bright constellations before you. They form a path that is unique to your Medicine, and you start receiving downloads of wisdom.

Turtle constellation appears, and as you soar through it, you affirm: *I am Creator.*

Thunderbird constellation appears, and as you soar through it, you affirm: *I am aligned in my nature and presence.*

Bear constellation appears, and as you soar through it, you affirm: *Rest is good Medicine.*

Deer constellation appears, and as you soar through it, you affirm: *I soften into self-love.*

Frog constellation appears, and as you soar through it, you affirm: *I am cleansed and purified.*

Butterfly constellation appears, and as you soar through it, you affirm: *I am transformed.*

Canada Goose constellation appears, and as you soar through it, you affirm: *We create equitable spaces.*

Porcupine constellation appears, and as you soar through it, you affirm: *I hold Ancestral knowing and connection.*

Crane constellation appears, and as you soar through it, you affirm: *I carry brilliant Medicine.*

Eagle constellation appears, and as you soar through it, you affirm: *I rise and soar in my leadership.*

Buffalo constellation appears, and as you soar through it, you affirm: *I am always supported.*

Wolf constellation appears, and as you soar through it, you affirm: *I am fiercely protected.*

Snake constellation appears, and as you soar through it, you affirm: *I am a Healer.*

Grandmother Spider creates the most gorgeous web you have ever seen, made of Stardust and sparkling bright. It transmutes into a healing vortex that surrounds you. All the healing from the journeys, Ceremonies, and reflections that you have moved through in this book gather here. You have remembered, reclaimed, and will now rise. This vortex becomes a healing cape, and on the back of it is a symbol representing the Medicine you carry in this world.

Fly back down to Earth and realign yourself with the Dreamcatcher that was waiting for you. Feel yourself now updating your energy and pour this into every part of your being. Stand tall. Claim your space here. Rise, beautiful soul, rise.

CELEBRATE

How often do you look back at how far you've come? How often do you celebrate your accomplishments? We are conditioned to meet our goals and then make new ones without taking time and space to celebrate and reflect. Most people say that we should take all the time we need to grieve, but what about taking as much time as we need to feel joy, excitement, and celebration?

When I received news that I got this book deal, it was the day before my birthday, in my favorite month of June. Two days later, my husband had a heart attack and was in the hospital for five days, alone because of COVID. I was frozen in fear that he wouldn't be okay, and as a result, my celebration was frozen, too! The excitement of the book deal was suppressed; there was no room for it to be felt, acknowledged, and celebrated. When folks in my local community started sharing the news of my book, I wanted to hide. I hadn't even celebrated it yet, and now the world was celebrating for me? I slowly thawed with healing work, but this experience showed me that celebration is another form of receiving. We can get blocked with trauma, and then there is no space for celebration to flow. If our nervous systems are overwhelmed, it's challenging to let the good things in and allow them to take up space.

A simple yet effective practice to make more room and clear trauma from our nervous systems is to shake. Over the years, I have practiced this on and off, but this year, I practiced it daily. I can share that at the time I am writing this it has been one year since I received this book deal, and I have so much more capacity and space to celebrate and receive now. The simple act of shaking my arms, my legs, my hands, and my whole body for a few minutes per day has opened me up to so many blessings. I encourage you to try it, too. There is no wrong way.

> **Medicine Reflection:** Take a moment to acknowledge how far you've come. What accomplishments or successes need to be celebrated?

MIRACULOUS HAPPENINGS

There is a beautiful Ceremony that I've had the privilege of attending called the Shaking Tent Ceremony—*Jiisikaan*—our oldest Ceremony as Ojibwe people. A ceremonial tent is placed on the Land, and the Medicine Person sits inside. They call on the Spirit World, and the tent begins to light up and shake. There are Animal sounds, Ancestor voices, whistles, and other noises that come through the tent. If I hadn't been there to see this with my own eyes, I wouldn't believe it. The tent is a space of dreaming and miracles. You ask the Medicine Person your question, and Spirit answers, offering you deep healing. I went to the first one with my dear friend Celeste. She was dreaming another baby into being but didn't know how it would happen, as her first pregnancy was complicated. When the tent shook, I saw a vision of a little girl run by, and the Medicine Person told her that she would indeed get pregnant again and all would be well. Today she has a two-year-old girl who is the brightest little soul and a miracle for her heart.

The Shaking Tents I have attended have reminded me of how intentional dreaming and ceremonial intention can create miracles. Sometimes I look at my children and remember that they were once a dream or a feeling in my heart. For me, they are evidence that miracles happen. What is your proof? If you need some inspiration, place your hand over your beating heart for you, my dear reader, are miraculous.

Spider Medicine Invocation

Dearest Spider, thank you for helping me to remember that I am the dream weaver of my life. Remind me of my resilience as I look back to celebrate all that I have accomplished. Amplify my energetic web with illumination, vitality, and magic. I am grateful for your teachings of patience as I allow space and time for my dreams to manifest. Help me to remember that miracles are all around, and I can tap into them anytime I am ready to dream my most beautiful life into being.

Mnidoons Giizis Moon Affirmation

As I fully embody the teachings of the 13 Moons, I stand tall and shine bright. I remember who I am, I reclaim the Medicines of the past, and I rise into what Creator dreamed for me. My wings are strong, my heart is full, and my Spirit is ready. I look up to you in the night Sky and co-create my greatest visions. I am ready. I am the Medicine.

○ ❭ ❭ ❭ ❭ ❭ ● ❰ ❰ ❰❰ ❰◯

SACRED SPACE CLOSING

The first time I walked into a studio to create a sacred atmosphere, I could feel my Ancestors filling the room. I remember softly drumming to them and singing a song to try to open up my throat. I prayed for the circle to hold me and remind me why I was there and what I was meant to do. As soon as the participants began to enter, a warmth came over the room. As they sat, I saw activation energy moving through the bodies and Spirits of all who were there. I saw the power that every person held in that space. Their wisdom informed me and their presence ignited me. Like you, they were Medicine Keepers.

This book has been a living, breathing energy of love, a portal and vortex of Creation. It is blessed by the Four Directions, the Moon, the Earth, the Sky, my Ancestors, Animal Spirits, and you. As we close this sacred space, may you remember that you matter. I see you, dear Creator, and it is a true blessing to walk each other home to the Cosmos. Together, with deep gratitude and reverence, we remember: *We are the Medicine.*

ENDNOTES

1. Ruchika Tulshyan and Jodi-Ann Burrey, "Stop Telling Women They Have Imposter Syndrome" *Harvard Business Review*, February 11, 2021, https://hbr.org/2021/02/stop-telling-women-they-have-imposter-syndrome.

2. Alexandra Eidens, *Big Life Journal for Kids* (Canada: Eidens, Inc., 2019).

3. Bob Joseph, *21 Things You May Not Know About The Indian Act* (Indigenous Relations Press, 2018).

4. Truth and Reconciliation Commission of Canada, "Honouring the Truth, Reconciling for the Future: Summary of the Final Report of the Truth and Reconciliation Commission of Canada," accessed October 12, 2021, https://nctr.ca/records/reports/.

5. Martha Henriques, "Can the legacy of trauma be passed down the generations?" *BBC Future*, March 26, 2019, https://www.bbc.com/future/article/20190326-what-is-epigenetics.

ACKNOWLEDGMENTS

I have always been the type of person who dives into a book by reading acknowledgments first. I love feeling into the web of connections of all of the people who help with its birth. Now that I have written one, I am deeply grateful for my co-creators. I couldn't have done this without you.

I am deeply grateful for the Land that helps to remind me that I belong. I acknowledge all that it carries and how that continues to inform me in my Medicine work in the world. I thank my Ancestors, known and unknown. Your words, visions, and dreamtime messages help me to keep going. *Miigwetch* for dreaming my essence into being. I hope I make you proud.

To my mother, my most treasured Elder. Thank you for holding a vision of my Medicine since I was a little girl. Your steady and continuous belief in me helps me birth new wings over and over again. I am grateful for your wisdom, connection, and advice in my writing. I'm eternally grateful that you were the first person to read and edit this book. To my father, thank you for dreaming a new way into being for your descendants. I treasure our time spent together on your home territory. It healed me more than you could ever know. To my sister—our memories of jumping off the dock into the Georgian Bay and walking on the rocks in our jelly shoes are imprinted in my heart forever. Thank you for being one of the most precious relationships of my life.

To my dear fam, Dave, Christina, Jacquie, Dieter, Tamara, Terry, and beyond—grateful for the type of support that only extended family can give. It means everything to me that my children are well loved by you. Celeste, Riki, Christine, Sandie, Aarti, Leslie, Heather, Julie, Brooke, Rose, Nicole, Lisa, Colette, Nic, Priya, Melissa—thank you for being my light. The friendship Medicine you offer me is pure magic. My close Indigenous kin, Jessica, Jacqui, Kaitlin, Shawna, Robyn, Monique—*Chi Miigwetch* for understanding me without me having to speak the words.

Marissa, thank you for helping me with my proposal edits. Since the moment we met, you have inspired me with your sparkle and brilliance. Delia, Kristin, and Jessica, thank you for being the best support during this wild pandemic time. You held things up for me that I couldn't. Kai, *Miigwetch* for the beautiful Turtle Medicine you infused into my pages and Steph, *Miigwetch* for the perfect cover art.

My dear teachers, mentors, and guides—a deep bow to you. To the Medicine People from the Anishinaabe, Algonquin, Q'ero, and other lineages, you have helped me remember my cosmic purpose. David Bedrick and Jeffrey Tambor, your Medicine continues to take me through birth and death cycles, so grateful we have met again in this lifetime. To all of the beautiful folks who have ever come to my healing space, sat in circle with me, shared my voice, and walked with me in unity. Every tear you have shed, every smile you have offered, every kind word you have gifted is imprinted in my soul. I would not be here without you. You are some of my greatest teachers.

To my editor, Allison, thank you for seeing my vision, deeply listening, and holding my words with compassion. I could not have asked for a better editing experience.

To the Hay House team, this book is a dream come true—one that I held close to my heart for over 20 years. I never imagined that my voice as an Indigenous Woman would land here or even be seen. This book is part of reconciliation for me, for that I am deeply grateful.

To the Spirits of the many children who were forgotten and powerfully came forward so the world could finally acknowledge them, I honor you. Miigwetch for lighting the Sky with orange on National Truth and Reconciliation Day, I will make sure you are never forgotten again.

Corey, Kai, and Elias, you are my Medicine in every way.

All my relations, *Gi-zaah'gi'in*—I love you.

ABOUT THE AUTHOR

Asha Frost (she/her) is an Indigenous Medicine Woman and a member of the Chippewas of Nawash First Nation. She is from the Crane Clan, the totem of leadership, and believes in holding space from vision and heart. As an energy healer, homeopath, and mentor, Asha has guided thousands of people through profound and lasting transformation.

Impacted by generational trauma and colonization, Asha has been on a lifelong journey of reclamation. A lupus diagnosis sent her on a path of studying and practicing a multitude of energy Medicine modalities with many guides. She has blended this life experience with her innate gifts and the wisdom of her Ancestors. She loves sharing her Medicine in powerful ways through Ceremonies, teachings, and speaking events. Through this work, she loves seeing people reclaim their roots, find their healing wisdom, and rise into their power.

Asha lives on Anishinaabe, Huron-Wendat, and Haudenosaunee Territory, with her husband and two beautiful children, with whom she co-creates a better world for the seven generations to come.

We hope you enjoyed this Hay House book. If you'd like to receive our online catalog featuring additional information on Hay House books and products, or if you'd like to find out more about the Hay Foundation, please contact:

Hay House, Inc., P.O. Box 5100, Carlsbad, CA 92018-5100
(760) 431-7695 or (800) 654-5126
(760) 431-6948 (fax) or (800) 650-5115 (fax)
www.hayhouse.com® • www.hayfoundation.org

———

Published in Australia by: Hay House Australia Pty. Ltd.,
18/36 Ralph St., Alexandria NSW 2015
Phone: 612-9669-4299 • *Fax:* 612-9669-4144
www.hayhouse.com.au

Published in the United Kingdom by: Hay House UK, Ltd.,
The Sixth Floor, Watson House, 54 Baker Street, London W1U 7BU
Phone: +44 (0)20 3927 7290 • *Fax:* +44 (0)20 3927 7291
www.hayhouse.co.uk

Published in India by: Hay House Publishers India,
Muskaan Complex, Plot No. 3, B-2, Vasant Kunj, New Delhi 110 070
Phone: 91-11-4176-1620 • *Fax:* 91-11-4176-1630
www.hayhouse.co.in

———

Access New Knowledge.
Anytime. Anywhere.

Learn and evolve at your own pace
with the world's leading experts.

www.hayhouseU.com

Hay House Titles of Related Interest

YOU CAN HEAL YOUR LIFE, the movie, starring
Louise Hay & Friends
(available as an online streaming video)
www.hayhouse.com/louise-movie

THE SHIFT, the movie,
starring Dr. Wayne W. Dyer
(available as an online streaming video)
www.hayhouse.com/the-shift-movie

***

*SECRETS OF SPACE CLEARING: Achieve Inner and Outer
Harmony through Energy Work, Decluttering, and Feng Shui,*
by Denise Linn

*PLANT WITCHERY: Discover the Sacred Language, Wisdom, and
Magic of 200 Plants,* by Juliet Diaz

MOONOLOGY: Working with the Magic of Lunar Cycles,
by Yasmin Boland

*AFRICAN GODDESS INITIATION: Sacred Rituals for Self-Love,
Prosperity, and Joy,* by Abiola Abrams

All of the above are available at your local bookstore,
or may be ordered by contacting Hay House (see next page).

***

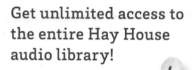